Another Perfect Piece

Monologues from Canadian Plays

Playwrights Canada Press
Toronto • Canada

Another Perfect Piece - Monologues from Canadian Plays
© Copyright 1995 Playwrights Canada Press
Playwrights Canada Press is the publishing imprint of
the Playwrights Union of Canada (PUC): 54 Wolseley St., 2nd fl.
Toronto, Ontario CANADA M5T 1A5
Tel: (416) 703-0201 Fax: (416) 703-0059
e-mail: cdplays@interlog.com   http://www.puc.ca

Playwrights Canada Press operates with the generous assistance
of The Canada Council - Writing and Publishing Section, and the
Ontario Arts Council.

Canadian Cataloguing in Publication Data
Main entry under title:
        Another perfect piece : monologues from Canadian plays

ISBN 0-88754-518-1
I. Monologues, Canadian (English). 2. Acting - Auditions
3. Canadian drama (English) - 20th century.* I. Hamill, Tony
PS8315.A56 1995   C812'.04508   C94-930884-6
PR9196.6.A56 1995

First edition: November, 1995. Second printing: June, 1997.
Printed and bound in Winnipeg, MB, Canada - Hignell Printing Ltd..

Table of Contents

Foreword

In 1990, Playwrights Canada Press published a collection of monologues from Canadian plays, *The Perfect Piece*, which has become our best-selling book in Canada and abroad.

The Perfect Piece has proven to be an invaluable tool for actors striving to showcase their talent in the audition and "get that part". But it has also proven to be a highly effective introduction to the wide range of Canadian plays for all kinds of readers — from drama students to artistic directors to readers simply interested in Canadian drama.

Since that time, many new, wonderful playwrights have emerged in this country. For this new collection, we have taken many monologues from these new writers and have also looked to many established playwrights — to both their new works and their proven 'hits' to present you with as wide a spectrum of monologues as possible. Much as we would like to, we simply can't represent every playwright in Canada in one book.

As you can see from perusing this book, the monologues are from many styles of play: dramatic and comedic, naturalistic and surrealistic, traditional and experimental, and everything in between. The book is divided into female and male sections, and in many cases women playwrights are writing parts for men and male playwrights are writing female roles. The pieces are arranged in a chronological order from young to old.

It is not our place to tell auditioning actors how to play these pieces. This is something they have to do themselves by reading the entire play to understand thoroughly the piece they are working on.

Then is the time to make choices about the part, and even take dramatic risks to "shine" and get the role.

You will notice, also, that we have not assigned approximate times to the monologues. We have tried to present monologues in many different lengths to suit many different audition needs. Each person reading or performing a piece will do it with different 'intentions' and perspectives and, as a result, at a different pace. Timing is individual. In a number of cases you will also notice that we have included much longer monologues that can easily be broken into two different audition pieces. This the actor must do carefully so as to maintain the story line, and the playwright's intention. As it is so important, we'll run the risk of being repetitive and say the only way to do this is to read the entire play. As I said in the original monologue collection, the artistic director you are auditioning for will know in an instant if you haven't read the play and understood the part.

If you like a particular piece, you could well find that there are many more in the play it was taken from, or in other plays by the same author. Almost all the pieces in this book are available from us at the Playwrights Union of Canada as books published by us or by other drama publishers, or as copyscripts — photocopied and cerlox-bound manuscripts. If we don't have the play in house we can contact the playwright. So give us a call.

And 'break a leg!'

Tony Hamill
Managing Editor

The Editors

Allegra Fulton has worked extensively as an actor across Canada on stage, film, radio and television. Acclaimed roles include Frida Kahlo in Gloria Montero's *Frida K.* (Tarragon Theatre), Michel Tremblay's *Counter Service* (Tarragon Theatre), Ariel Dorfman's *Death and the Maiden*, James Nichol's *The Stone Angel* (created role of Arlene for the Theatre Passe Muraille - Blyth Festival world premiere) and Judith Thompson's *The Crackwalker* (Critics Award for best actress). Allegra was nominated for a Dora Mavor Moore Award for outstanding performance in *Nocturnal Emissions* in 1991. Screen credits include "Thirty-two Short Films About Glenn Gould" and Deny Arcand's section of "Montreal Vu Par..."

Tony Hamill is the Managing Editor at Playwrights Canada Press, and the editor of *The Perfect Piece - Monologues from Canadian Plays*, *You're Making a Scene - Scenes from Canadian Plays*, and *Six Canadian Plays*. A member of the Canadian Actors' Equity Association, he studied acting at the HB Studio in New York City for four years, including one year with Uta Hagen. In addition to theatre work in the Toronto area, he recently appeared in Sally Clark's film, "The Art of Conversation". He is the author of *Consider the Lillies*, a play about Beatrice Lillie's formative years growing up and performing in Toronto.

Jon Kaplan is the theatre editor at Toronto's *NOW* Magazine, where he has worked since the first issue in 1981. A recipient of The Brenda Donohue Award for his contribution to Toronto theatre, Jon is also a correspondent for the London-based *Plays International* and the New York-based *Theater Week*, and reports regularly on theatre for CJRT - FM radio.

Timing

As each individual actor will read and perform a piece at his or her own pace depending on how they want to present the monologue, we have not assigned times to the pieces. We have found that one typeset page can run anywhere from 1 minute : 10 seconds to 1:20 or even 2:00. So we recommend that you time the pieces you are interested in auditioning with, for your own timing.

Availability

The majority of the monologues in this books are taken from plays that are directly available from the Playwrights Union of Canada (PUC) either as plays published by Playwrights Canada Press, published by another Canadian drama publisher, or available as a copyscript — a photocopied, cerlox-bound manuscript. In some cases a monologue may have been written by a playwright who is not a member of PUC, who has not sent us the script. In that case, you can still contact us and we will pass on your request for the entire script to the author.

Copyright

All the monologues in this book can be used in auditions without the need to obtain permission. Please note that the monologues and the plays from which they are extracted may not be performed before a paying audience without the permission of the author or his or her authorized agent. For information on obtaining both amateur and professional production rights to these plays please contact PUC at 54 Wolseley Street, 2nd floor, Toronto, Ontario M5T 1A5, tel: (416) 703-0201, fax: (416) 703-0059.

Women

$\mathcal{F}$inal $\mathcal{D}$ecisions (War)

Guillermo Verdecchia

Monica has been "disappeared" and tortured. She is in a cramped, wet, dark cell. She will die under interrogation in the next scene.

MONICA

One. One, two.

In the Nazi camps, the prisoners would try to get jobs in the laundry or the kitchen. And they would perform little acts of sabotage. Insignificant acts like burning a shirt. Here, there are no laundries or kitchens. Sabotage is almost impossible.

One, two, three.

This is a machine that makes animals. They put us in here and tell us to moo instead of talk.

In the morning, it's almost better to be an animal. The guard comes by and sometimes he speaks to me. He is a stupid brute. I have begun to hope that he will stay a little longer and speak to me for a while. When he offered me a cigarette I almost cried. I mustn't begin to believe he is my friend.

One, two, three, four.

There was someone in this block who could whistle like a bird. Every night she would whistle and we would tap very quietly on the walls when she was finished. And she — I don't know if it was a woman but I like to think so — she would whistle a little more. I'd fall asleep to her whistling.

Whistling, tapping, scratching our names in the wall, counting out loud are the only acts of sabotage available to us. And they are sabotage because they laugh in the face of brutality.

Cows can't count.

One, two, three, four, Five.

***

Available as a copyscript.

Rags and Dreams

Peggy Sample

Elizabeth is a young woman of seventeen, living in Canada in the 1800s.

ELIZABETH

I'm planning my bridal quilt. I guess you can say I've been planning it my whole life. Well, that's a girl's hope, isn't it? To find someone wonderful and get married and have children and keep your household. It's either that or stay an old maid and keep someone else's household — your parents' or your brother's — ugh. When you get married, it's your own place, yours and your husband's.

Anyway, last night Daniel James walked me home from Marie LeBlanc's quilting party. The stars were twinkling down like they were laughing their joy at us, and the moon was so bright we could see our shadows. It was very romantic! We got to the old orchard and sat down on a blanket of apple blossoms, their scent heavy in the air. And he said, "So you told me last month when I was seeing you home from Mrs. Merryweather's bee that you'd just finished piecing your twelfth quilt. Have you started a new one yet?" I replied, "Now Daniel James, you know very well a girl can't start her thirteenth quilt without being engaged to be married or she never will be asked!" He smiled, took my hands in his, and said in a low, husky voice, "Would you like to start on your thirteenth quilt, Elizabeth?" Like a fool, I just looked at him. until he said, even softer, "One to share with me?" I thought I was going to faint. My breath was coming so fast, my heart was racing, and my skin was so hot, but I looked down, I sat very still and I said, "I have been looking for something to stitch." I looked in his eyes then, and they were as blue and shining as the night sky...

***

Available as a copyscript.

My Secret Hiding Place

Marium Carvell

A teen-aged girl hides from her father in the basement during school hours.

FLOWER

I need time to think. Why can't people understand that I need time to myself sometimes? And this new teacher we got at school is the worst. He doesn't understand what's going on with me at all. Okay, I'm not like other children. I know that. He expects me to live up to this stupid name my parents gave me; Flower. What were they thinking? People are much too expectant of a name like Flower. They all think you must be the most delicate girl in the world with a slender delicate face, ruby red lips, rosy high cheekbones, clean clear eyes with lashes till next Tuesday, and a slender body with a waist that would snap if you squeezed it too hard. Well, I have a fat face, fat cheeks, bloodshot eyes, boring lashes, and I love to eat. So, the danger of anyone snapping my waist is very slim -- which I know I'm not. But being different doesn't mean I should be ostracized from the community. I'm not a witch. I'm just a pudgy girl who grasps things faster than the normal child, that's all. Gifted, such a stupid word. It's not a gift to be so smart — it's a curse. Maybe it wouldn't be so bad if my stupid teacher didn't keep calling my Dad and letting him know every new thing that astonishes him about me. It only makes my Dad hate me even more.

Just be yourself. I hate those three words. My body is full of different selves. How can I be myself, if I haven't found myself yet? Just once, it would be nice to act like the type of airhead who asks what the name of the team with the pretty uniforms is. Hey furnace, I think that when people tell you to just be yourself, what they really mean to say is: Please be as boring as possible, and don t embarrass me, okay?
I can't help it if my Dad is so insecure about his lack of education that he feels I'm a threat to him. Stupid man. (*beat*).
Oh-oh. Dad is still here. Why hasn't he gone yet? Something must be wrong. Maybe he's onto me, But, I'm almost positive he didn't hear me

come back in this morning. I can't let him find me here. Okay, I'll just have to be very quiet until he decides it's time to leave. It's starting to get really warm behind here. I wish I could go out there and confront Dad, and not be afraid to face whatever punishment he has to dish out. But right now, that doesn't sound like too much fun. I've had enough pain for one day. I think I'll just stay put. Right here where I know I'm warm.

Oh no. He's getting too close for comfort. He'll never find me here, though. Can't catch me, I'm the gingerbread man. Come on, Flower, think evil thoughts and cast him away with your mind. Go to work, old man. Go away, and let me have some peace for a change. No more footsteps. Maybe he got my message. I hope so. Still no footsteps. He must be gone. Or is he just waiting for me to come out? Oh God. I feel like my head is being put in a vise, and being crushed until it explodes, my intestines all in knots. That's how you make me feel, old man. He just makes me so nervous all the time. I can't do anything right for him. How can a girl be so smart, and not be able to figure out a way for her Dad to love her? It doesn't make any sense. Can you figure that one out for me, furnace?

***

Taken from a CBC Morningside Radio Drama.

The Hope Slide

Joan MacLeod

During one night in 1990 in the Kootenays, a remote and mountainous area 400 miles east of Vancouver, Irene travels from 1962 to 1967, from North Vancouver to the Doukhobor prison outside the town of Hope, from the turbulent Kootenays of the Sixties to the other side of Hope where a mountain collapsed in 1965.

IRENE

First off I want it made perfectly clear that reporting to you, Miss Toye, a truant officer-slash-psychologist, is a complete violation of my rights and all I hold sacred and dear. The form in front of you was signed under duress, a condition of my being allowed back into school that I was forced to agree to. I was backed into a corner, the pen practically jammed into my hand. Although I am not against education *per se* I believe attendance should be voluntary.

My understanding, Miss Toye, is that I am to report to and talk to you, my truant officer-slash-warden, personally, once a month and that if I am absent from school without a phone call and note from my mother or the Queen Mother or God himself then I am going to be expelled again. I agree to these conditions although it is with a heavy heart that I am agreeing. I also agree to keep my clothes on at all times, even in gym class I will wear my shorts over my stupid dress to avoid causing any further rioting amongst the members of my class. But although I am no longer allowed to protest publicly, I want you to know Mary Kalmakoff, Harry Kootnikoff and Paul Podmorrow are still heroes to me, unsung martyrs whose song I intend to keep alive come hell or high water.

These were real people who died an unjust and horrible death. How'd you like a mountain to fall on your head, Miss Toye? Or a bomb to explode in your lap. How'd you like to go on a hunger strike to get publicity but once you died nobody paid attention? The newspaper didn't even say it was sad. And this is absolutely the saddest thing that I think has ever happened but I do digress.

I would like you to write down right now that I, Irene Dickson, am absolutely thrilled to be back in school and that the idea of doing grade nine all over again is extremely exciting to me. I am turning over a new leaf, knuckling under; and disappointment is no longer a part of my life. I see this September as a new starting point on the rocky and difficult road of the life of me — Irene Dickson. You got all that?

What are you writing down? Everything on the form in front of you is totally true...except the part about my parents being divorced. It was an experiment I devised to see if people treat you any better if you come from a broken home. They don't. My parents get on like a house on fire, always have. The part about future occupation is true: dancer-slash-actress-slash-mayor of a great city. Present occupation: spirit wrestler. Meanness and forgiveness are growing inside me at an equal rate and creating an unholy war.

If you're going to write stuff down about me I think it is my right to see it...Does it say there I have these theories? i.e. — last year I predicted North Van was going to slide into the ocean and settle like Atlantis under the Lion's Gate Bridge. I also have several theories on hitchhiking, sex and friendship, drunken boys, the end of the world and, of course, the Doukhobors. Take your pick.

Okay don't take your pick. Wanna talk about sex? No problem, anything goes here, I am an open book. Perhaps you are under the mistaken impression, along with the rest of this place, that Walter Dewitt is my boyfriend. That Walter Dewitt and I are doing it. Well, we're not. I do not see Walter in that way. He is my friend, my best friend, as a matter of fact, my only friend. You know Walter. He is very skinny and very bright, highly goofy. And like myself highly persecuted — my tribe. Walter and I believe friendship is the absolute highest state of being.

(*pause*)

I like your hair. I believe women should have long hair, another one of my theories. In pre-historic times our hair was long so that babies, our babies, could hold on while we ran through the trees being chased by God knows what. Babies are born knowing how to hold but now they've lost it and have to be taught. No. They come out knowing but then they forget and have to be taught. I don't know. But something has happened with regard to babies and their ability to hold on in this century.

I don't mean I don't ever think about sex. I think about it often. Perhaps constantly. Not the actual act of sex which is as yet unknown to me but I do think of my policies regarding sex: i.e. — do everything but, you know, as many times as you want with whoever you want just keep your hymen intact. When I first learned of my hymen and the importance of keeping it untouched, in place, I imagined it this big shield I could hold out front and ward off guys with, rather like a Viking would have. It's a great word, hymen — hymn and amen and hyena all rolled into one. This big bouncy kangaroo thing that laughs its guts out. I mean I know it isn't that and I know it isn't something that you carry with a spear but I used to also worry that my time will come, I will meet him and it will be perfect and holy and wild but...what if my hymen didn't break? What if guys just sort of bounced off it? This tough old piece of skin pulled tight as a drum, a bongo drum barring the way to heaven.

What if it leaves men in pain? Pain is something they cannot bear nearly as well as us. They also have a great deal of trouble touching their own eyes.

Don't write that down! Just write down stuff like I am knuckling under. I love that kind of crap. I am knuckling under. I know, I know. Our time is up. Tell me about it.

***

Published by Coach House Press.

By a Thread

Diane Flacks

'Astro-projecting', bluesy grandmothers, irrational fears, hidden secrets and flying paint — welcome to Rosie's way out.

> *ROSIE is armed with a paint brush which she hooks into her pants, and a can of paint. She uses the fourth wall as an imaginary mural which she is painting.*

ROSIE

I don't want to make *fire art* I want to be a rock star!

But I can't play the guitar because of my Uncle Joe and his Longshoreman hands broke my fucking wrist! Fuuuuck!

I started leaving my body at a really young age. 10 or 12. When he moved in. Of course my body was mostly wearing navy blue cords faded at the knees and inner thighs, brown acrylic sweaters, and a hair band...so it's not hard to understand why my body was so easy to leave.

You know that place? That dark twitchy pre-dream place where you see colours and flashing lights and your grade three teacher all covered in Jello? I love that place...Well, so, every so often I would feel this...presence there...this presence standing there in my room watching me...and I knew...that it was bad. And then this...feeling came oozing into my room through the cracks in the floor, through the vents, through the window. Thick as mud as he stood there...smiling — smiling. And I'd tuck my sheets in really tight around me, but it didn't matter. And he must have heard my heart pounding right out of my chest. Because you know what? Did you know that when you're scared your heart doesn't pound faster, it pounds louder? It's true. That's why they say that dogs can smell fear. They don't SMELL fear...they hear it.

And I just wanted to get the hell out of there, astro-project over to my Fairy Godmother's house...

...but I couldn't, I couldn't, I couldn't, so I had to stay up here, watching. (*motioning to a space above her*)

And I couldn't get mad at him because he was the last of the Longshoremen. And my Mother's biggest fear was being alone. And she wasn't alone. And so I learned how to leave my body...I used to do it all the time. I don't do it so much now. When I'm alone, walking on the street at night. At the bank machine...at the Eaton Centre...at the subway!...When I hear that sound!...When I see that smile!...When I get that FEELING! You know that feeling? It's like...

(*stops, softly, a discovery*) It's a feeling.

ROSE stands and dips a paint brush from her belt in a paint on the floor. Note: the paint can is full of water. She slowly approaches her mural. Her knees begin to buckle. She stops, puts her hand on her chest and speaks quietly to herself .

Stay.

Do you think I could stay in my body for the rest of my life if I could just find something to paint, that I didn't want to burn?

***

*Published by Playwrights Canada Press in
"Singular Voices - Plays in Monologue Form".*

Ghetto

James O'Reilly

The causes and effects of urban economic ghettoization are explored by tracking the lives of three residents of a government housing complex which has failed miserably.

BRIGIT has just woken, screaming from a bad dream. she goes to a table and lights a cigarette.

BRIGIT

What if Mozart was born in the ghetto? What if, okay, Mozart Junior. Say he's a snotty teenager...awkward...hands and head too big for his body the way boys get. Screamin' white friggin' ponytail and everything...and he's got this power in his hands just dyin' to get out...dyin' to work itself out on little old ivories. But where's he gonna see a piano in the ghetto, right?

So, what does he do with this power...gotta come out right? So he becomes a champ at jimmyin' locks and undoin' bra-straps'n fiddly stuff like that. One thing leads to another and eventually he becomes a B & E king. And he's good at it, great at it...no job too tough for a genius.

Anyway, he's on a job one night. Big house — ya know the type — island in the kitchen 'n stuff. His partner Buddy's upstairs goin' through the drawers for cash. Mozart Junior's standing lookout at the window...thinkin' about this pain he's got in his head that won't go away and how his life is shit, and how he's gotta do somethin' more with his hands or he's gonna blow up. He doesn't know where this feelin's comin' from but it's there...and he can't ignore it. He starts gappin' out. Buddy's trashin' the bedroom. Junior's gappin'. Buddy's trashin'. Junior's gappin'. Trashin' and gappin'. Then, Junior snaps completely. Downs a crystal decanter full of old scotch in a gulp, then tosses it into the fireplace and starts to look around the house. There's a piano in the sunroom by the garden...sure, why not?...a grand piano in the oriental sunroom.

Junior heads for the piano. Never seen one before in person. But as soon as his fingers touch the keys his head becomes clear. He's talkin' to God. Makin' masterpieces in his mind. Thinkin' about paintings of exotic fruit and French bread on black satin. He feels the sun on his face. Everything around him becomes transparent. Crystal clear. He plays passionate beautiful music...and for a second he is music. And it's all perfect...'cept Buddy's downstairs now and the neighbours got their lights on 'n Buddy can hear police sirens. So he starts smackin' Junior in the face sayin'..."Are you nuts? Let's go! But, uh-uh, Junior keeps right on playin', paintin' a masterpiece with his brain. Buddy hates music. He thinks, "This guy's fucked. He's gonna rat on me for sure." So he clubs Junior over the head with a piece of pipe he always carries with him, and... Junior dies right there on the floor. Mozart dies at the piano for the first time. Mozart dies a stone's-throw away from the ghetto...with half a masterpiece painted in his brain.

(*languidly*) Yea...mow-zart...art...art...art-schmart...art-schmart...

***

Available as a copyscript.

Playballs

Mark Brownell

Lucy is a woman of 25-35 years of age. Here she talks about one of her first experiences umpiring in a professional league.

LUCY

Florida always had a pretty good team. But, like everyone else, the players didn't know what to make of a woman umpire. During the games they'd call me "Ma'am" and "Miss." Didn't bother me. I been called worse. Things were going pretty well with me and the Gators but then...

This was the game. I was behind the plate. Inning after inning passed without me missing a pitch. There wasn't one complaint from either bench. Had ol' Karl seen me that day, he would have bumped me to the head of the class. I was awesome...until the bottom of the ninth.

(*watching the hits from behind the plate*) They hit every pitch. A single here. A triple to the wall. A home run. All of a sudden it was "rabbit ball." The score was getting tighter and tighter — as was my sphincter. When is this game going to end? A single. Another double. What a pressure cooker!

With two outs, bases loaded, and the Gators behind by only one run, I can't take this anymore. I got the sweats. In steps the batter...

(*she bears down, calling balls and strikes*) Baaw. Steerriiike! Baaaw. Streeriiike! Baaw. He works the count to 3 and 2. Two out — bases loaded. Time takes a weird twist. Gets all bent out of shape like. In comes the pitch, a fastball — but to me it's just floating there like a leather zeppelin — shoulder high — up and in at his head — maybe above his head...catcher gets a hernia trying to get it in the mitt. The batter watches it pass — as he should have — and without a second's hesitation, I yell "SSTTEE~RIII~KE!"

I knew it was a ball, but I had wanted a strike. Everything was back in real time. I blew it.

(*as batter*) You suck! You really suck!
(*as herself*) Shut up!
(*as manager*) That is the worst call I have ever seen in my thirty years of coaching!. You lost the game for us! You suck! You suck! You suck!

Everybody was furious, and rightly so. I choked, pure and simple. As I walked off the field, they kept following me, hemming me in — which, for some strange reason, made me think of what Karl always preached to us: "The key to success is a good eye, an even temper, and being the boss of your game. You should also know where the nearest exit is. And remember to tell the scorekeeper where you want the body sent."

My career — what there was of it — was finished. I got fired for one bad call — but it was the most important call.

***

Available as a copyscript.

Seeds

Edward Roy

"Seeds" follows the tangled relationship of a struggling actor, his New Age girlfriend, Bethanne, a bitter theatre critic, and his alcoholic wife. It is about the desire to have children in a world on the brink of The Apocalypse.

> *BETHANNE is holding a condom full of water and a pin.*

BETHANNE

When I was a little girl I used to say, "I'm going to have ten children when I grow up". The first time I told my mother that she laughed so hard she fell off her chair. As I grew up the only girl in a brood of five, I realized why my mother found my desire to have ten children so hysterical. Watching her endure a messy divorce and all the sacrifices she had to make to maintain the clan through two recessions made the thought of having children evaporate from my mind. That's why I thought Laurence and I were a match made in heaven. We were in love. Successful. He was strong, sophisticated and had no desire to have children. I had a great portfolio. Didn't take a bath on Black Monday. Everything seemed fine but I wasn't happy. I began to get restless. I was trying to figure out what was missing from my life when one of the credit clerks on my floor got pregnant. I've always enjoyed the little time I spend with my nieces and nephews. And my brothers' wives are always warning me not to wait too long or it will be too late. There is always someone around encouraging me to have children. So I thought having a baby might not be such a bad thing. When I first mentioned it to Laurence he blanched. He ranted. He argued. And finally we agreed to wait awhile and he promised if I felt the same way in a year he'd reconsider. That was two years ago. So when I brought it up this morning I might as well have said let's axe murder your mother. Tempting thought. I guess you can't expect a person to change. But I think you have to be philosophical about life.

Accidents can happen. (*holding a pin to the condom*) Sometimes it's fate and sometimes...(*putting holes in the condom*) a person is overwhelmed with temptation. And there are so many temptations in life. You have to pick the ones you're going to succumb to very carefully because you can't be controlled by your desires can you? I mean if a person were to succumb to every desire they had in life...regardless of agreements they've made with other people, what would be left of their self respect? What kind of world would we be living in? (*looking at the empty condom*) Still, I'm tempted.

***

Available from the author - contact Playwrights Union of Canada.

Caveman Rainbow

Caroline Gillis

Marie-Lissa, is a woman in her early 30s struggling with the possibility that she may have cancer. In this speech she expresses her frustration over the impossibilities she has coped with in her life; and her anger with the class structure that keeps people down.

MARIE-LISSA

Emil doesn't believe in true love.
So he says.
But if that's true, how come he spends all his money on fashion clothes and getting his hair dyed a different colour every week? And how come he's got that special bank account so he can get his eyes lifted or tucked or pulled or whatever?

I think his eyes are fine.
I think his eyes are beautiful.
But Emil says, "I'm not trying to look younger. I'm just trying to stay the same."
How come people are so scared of getting old?
For some people getting old would be a prize.
It's just skin, after all.
If I had that money I'd do something self-improving.
Like one time I almost went to live with a family in Quebec to learn French, but I couldn't because I didn't finish high school, and I was too old for the bursary program, so I'd have to pay for it myself, unless of course I'd been on unemployment for six months prior to the course, in which case I'd be entitled to a bursary, but I'd have to take high-school upgrading at Continuing Ed., which I'd have to pay for myself unless I'm over sixty-five. Then it would be free.
Then I could quit my job, wait eight weeks, go on unemployment for six months, and then I could take the course.
Shit.

You gotta be under twenty-five or over sixty-five to use a friggin'
HELP LINE in this city.
I can't even rent a VCR in my own neighbourhood like a normal
human being. To rent a VCR I've got to give the guy a credit card or
three-hundred dollars.
But I can rent a video by just giving him a phone number.
So I can get the video but no VCR.
What am I supposed to do with the video?
Throw it on top of the TV and hope for the best.
And even if I said what the hell, and even if I had three hundred dollars
in my bank account, I couldn't take it out anyway because someone at
the bank decided that I was only allowed to take out sixty dollars a day
on my CONVENIENCE CARD.
Every person behind a counter or a desk is the same person.
You look at the Post Office some time.
Don't they all look related to you?
No wonder there's so much unemployment these days.
There's only one person got the same desk job all across the whole
country.
No wonder my mother never owned a car and I never owned a car, and
my kids, if I had any, would never own a car.
There's someone out there afraid we might just drive right out of our
place in society.
I could always rent a car I guess, but to do that I need a credit card, a
full-time job and my name in the white pages of the phone book for a
full year.
Shit.
I mean, basically, right now I've got absolutely nothing.
No kids, no husband, no car, no VCR. But...I've got great hair.

What if I were bald?

*** ,

Published by Coach House Press in "Solo".

The Ascension of Anais Nin

Wanda Graham

It's Paris in the Thirties. Anais Nin discovers the 'gangster-hobo-author', Henry Miller. He discovers her seducing Antonin Artaud in church. She finds his jealousy laughable.

ANAIS

I married once. That was like falling asleep in prison. I don't want to be pissed on! You think to choke the life out of me that will stop me...or the wagging of my tongue? Even if you tear me to bits, scatter my words to the four directions, you can't throw me far enough. Like Jason's teeth, like my sex, we will spring to life again. The others, the thousands, will rise around you and scream my revenge.

Man. You wimp. You sad sad sliver of fearful nature, begging only for a place to hide...a place to lick and piddle in darkness and shame.

I gave you what you wanted. Each and every one of you. I was not afraid. Look. Look at my shining face, my arms of steel, my teeth that sever cleaner than a knife...you saw me sunder the cords of my little girl's life and you pissed with fear...you feel my tremendous love and tremble with weakness...you hear my anger and poke at me with fingers...you little dull knife you...I weep and all women weep with me, I dream and there are storms at sea, I drum and the universe thunders! You, writer! Recorder of the facts, orderer of things. What made you think you were a ready match for the LOVE, THE GODDESS, VENUS, THE UNIVERSE? Hmmmm? I did! The truth? I am life itself. That is what I write about. That is what has brought me to cracked bones and rivers of blood. And I rise above you, and your spurt of small blood. You, rubbing and rubbing till the nub of you disappears back into the sand. And you won't even notice your own demise.

I will have all the love I need!

***

Available from author - contact Playwrights Union of Canada.

Connie in Egypt

Stewart Lemoine

Connie is a Canadian librarian who travels to Egypt, more or less on a whim.

CONNIE

You're standing in line at a museum and you've been there for a while. It's a busy day and they're only admitting a few people at a time. You're very close to getting in, when all of a sudden the couple in front of you is now joined by two other couples and they all get admitted and you're now going to have to wait another fifteen minutes before it'll be your turn. You know you should say something, but you don't. Why not?

Is it because these other couples are incorrigibly stupid and it's pointless to waste your perceptions on them? Or is it because they might yell at you and make you cry? Are you afraid of seeming really desperate to get into the museum when in fact you're just killing time and your objections are about principle anyway? Those two couples were late because they lingered over breakfast, enjoying their time in one another's company. You arrived early because you are alone. Alone alone alone.

If only you could impale them all as a group, just jam a pole through the six of them and sort of swing them off around a corner. But you can't. You seethe instead. Or, you do what I do and think happy thoughts. Like what?

Well, in my thoughts, the three heedless couples are admitted to the museum. They follow the prescribed route for seeing absolutely everything in the shortest possible time. In a great hall, they stand in contemplation of one of the minor temples of antiquity. Suddenly, abruptly, one of the stone support columns gives way and the roof of the edifice slides forward and falls, crushing the legs of the three women and effectively confining them to wheelchairs for the rest of their lives.

There's no cause for this mishap, save the steady weakening of the pillars over a period of two or three thousand years. This temple was always going to fall at the time that it did. Nonetheless, the three couples sue the museum for negligence in failing to anticipate the calamity and they receive substantial settlements. Their lives are never the same though, and only one of the marriages actually grows stronger as a result of these hardships. Another ends quickly in divorce, and the third drags on for thirty years, slowly becoming a festering morass of resentment, infidelity, alcoholism, and assisted suicide.

And the one thing they all keep thinking, though not one of them will ever say it out loud, is, "If only we'd gone into the museum a little later. If only we'd waited fifteen more minutes." Well ya didn't, did ya?

Like I say, happy thoughts make everything just fine.

***

Available from author - contact Playwrights Union of Canada.

Bivouac

Louise Arsenault

On the eve of graduating from the Crossroads rehab, Judith is shocked to learn that it is closing down and that the job her beloved counsellor Greg promised her is non-existent. Her only real shelter from her ravaged life now becomes the truth itself as she finally reveals to her belligerent roommate why she has lived her life in a cocoon of protective flesh.

JUDITH

I'm not stupid only slow (*speaking as her uncle*) "Eating Smarties don't make you a smarty, stupid. Come here, you don't look so smart with your tunic up over your head on a Milky Way crate. I'm counting each Smartie that's missing, better not open your mouth 'cept for candies, say nothing to your mother about it.

But I can't...I can't talk good. My mouth's covered up with his free hand and, and he says if I like it so much he's gonna give me all I want. I can't say nothing to no one cause they won't hear anyway. "I'm too small, too small for...that, Uncle Hubbie." But his big red thing's tearing into me and I'm on the Milky Way crate not listening to him breathing funny anymore, no. All I can hear is Gran Vi reciting that poem to me like on that day. And all I can see are those stars she taught me...And that's all I want to see cause he's making those sounds he's got and he's putting it in me again and again, and my head's hitting down on the crates, and my brain's spilling...spilling out on the cellar floor, like one of them cherry blossoms.

Daddy came down and he seen what Uncle Hubbie did to me. That was the day he got his brain exhausted in the garage. When I was sewed up and came back from the hospital it started up again. Daddy just sat there watching in the cellar like a root vegetable cause he knew Uncle owned the place and he did it to my mother too.

(*pause*) It's like I had this big bruising in me every time he did it to me, only it was in my feelings. Chocolate weren't enough anymore to make it numb. Each time the bruise got bigger, I had some liquor till I got sick in the head with it, screamin', "I'll never go down there in that cellar even if you make me." but I couldn't be any help to my mother in the dépanneur no more and that's when they sent me off. They gave me the shock cause they got me in the wing for crazies. (*pause*) I don't know how many times they gave it to me.

***

Available as a copyscript.

2 Incarnations of Siva

David Augustine Fraser

24-year-old Katy, synthesizes 2 ideas: she expresses a budding writer's confident awareness of personal identity and, at the same time, she finds voice for the near-mythic fears which threaten her marriage. Here, she is talking to her husband Geoffrey, on their honeymoon.

KATY

There was a tree out back, past our beech forest. My father tightened coils of barbed wire around it, to support a fence. I named that tree, then and there: I called it *my* maple tree. No-one sat under it but me. The tree grew, and the fence stood. (*slight pause*) The wire tightened. (*slight pause*) Every summer I could hear the pitch of the wire, when you strike it, get higher, until it made a squealing sound when the tree rocked in the wind, like a mouse caught in a trap...I stood by that tree and watched the wire cut deeper into its living...(*searching for the word*)...cambium. Cambium. And listened to it screaming like it was trying to tear up its roots. Before we married, I went back; I took the beech forest trail out to the tree. I couldn't believe my eyes! Geoffrey, the fence is still standing, on either side, but it's been lifted up from the ground — like an old woman hitching her skirts, or the entrance to an abandoned circus — a horse can walk under it. My little maple tree is 50 feet high! And the wire is lost inside! The tree has swallowed it up...there's a ring of metal tight around its heart. It will be there for years, through storms, through generations of birds — until it dissolves away, or my tree dies...

Pause.

I know a woman whose wedding ring has been cutting into her finger for 37 years. Her flesh had grown back and healed over the ring. Nothing man-made is more binding that that ring. (*slight pause*) They tie wire — around trees — to kill them? Doesn't always work, though. Not with this one.

Her right hand unconsciously touches her ring finger.

***

Available from the author - contact Playwrights Union of Canada.

No Cycle - Still

Harry Standjofski

In a series of 5 plays based on Zen Buddhist techniques of Japanese Noh theatre, the author makes profound statements about life, about avoiding the traps of our own making. In this piece, Viv, a young woman, is talking to Lily, a slightly older woman who has just discovered she has cancer.

VIV

Well, if being sick makes you look that good...I look like shit today, right? I got like no sleep last night. Oh, last night, last night. I got my period last night. In a cab. I have no cycle, eh? The things just slurps out unexpectedly three or four times a year. I've saved a mint in birth control. Anyway, I'm in a cab, I look down, and blech. My dress was a mess and the poor guy's cab...I didn't have the guts to tell him. What a disaster.

I went out with this guy last night — well, I've sort of been seeing him on and off — but last night was our first foray into the realm of the senses. He's an older guy, a lot older, ha. A dentist — lots of money. Very distinguished looking. Divorced looking, you look at him and you know he's divorced. We met at a party at my parents' place, for Christ's sake. He shows up at the gallery the next day, takes me out, spoils me to death. I'm so stupid. I don't really like the guy, you know, he's all right. Well, you want to take me out and spend lots of money on me, fine — I'm going to refuse? Anyway, this has been going on, I don't know, a month, two months. So last night he takes me out to see this play — real piece of shit — some intense family drama about life in rural Canada; it literally took place in the kitchen. So afterwards we go for sushi and we're eating and drinking and he, he starts talking all seriously, you know? He's never talked like...I mean, up to now it's been a lot of small talk, but tonight, tonight it's the full treatment. The Divorce, and a long time on that one. The sense of failure. Thirty years as a dentist. He said...he said, I feel like I have been standing still watching my life walk past me. Yeah...

And I don't want to hear this stuff, right? I mean, I'm doing well — no, that's not what I mean. I mean, it's all right to have some nice chit-chat over dinner and then watch him puff around the dance floor, but I don't want to hear this stuff about failure. So I'm drinking as much as he'll pay for, right? And I'm saying these obnoxious things, making smart-ass remarks about everything he says and I can tell I'm hurting his feelings, but I can't stop myself and he's trying to pretend like it's not bothering him.

Anyway, we go to his place and you have to see this place. His wife got the house, right? So, he's bought himself this renovated condo on St. Paul, but he's decorated it all Japanese with no chairs, just these cushions on the floor and the midget tables and the erotic drawings. And the piano. And on the piano there's this photo of a woman, like a real knockout, so I ask, "Who's this? Another conquest?" "No," he says, "that's my daughter." She's older than me, right? She's a lawyer.

So we're on the floor, and he's talking all serious again and I could tell he was really nervous, which really bugged me for some reason. It's because...well, I'm starting to realize that he really likes me. And he's opening his heart and I'm making fun of him and I can see he's hurt, but I can't stop...Finally I kissed him just to shut myself up.

But it was worse in bed. First of all, he's really nervous or he comes from a strange old school of fucking I've never heard of. And taking this big tired old dick into your mouth...Touching him was weird, his back...I mean, he has a really good body for a guy his age...He tried to drag an orgasm out of me, practically tore my boobs off at one point. Anyway, it's over and I'm hoping I can sleep, but no, it starts — you know when guys talk late at night? They're so glad it's dark and you can't see them and they take out this quiet little voice — they all have that same voice — and they tell you how the world has misinterpreted their dreams.

But I couldn't stay awake. I started having this dream. It was weird: I was on a beach, it was winter, it was really cold, it's night and I'm on this beach watching this turtle, this huge turtle dragging itself towards the sea.

Then he asks me a question, but I'm watching my turtle, right? So I say WHAT? And he laughs and hugs me and I thought "Oh, no, he wants to fuck me again" but he didn't. He just gives me a kiss on the forehead, says good night and rolls over.

But now I can't sleep. I started trembling all over, I couldn't stop. I didn't want him to notice, but the more I tried to stop, the worse it got and he asks "Is anything wrong?" and I spring from the bed. I just made it to the can. I puked my guts out. And I'm in his bathroom, naked, wiping the rim of the bowl with toilet paper and the light comes on and I yell "TURN IT OFF" and it dies. And my eyes get used to the dark and this silhouette of an old naked man is in the doorway asking "Are you all right?"

Then it's me running around getting dressed, trying not to look at him in his kimono and saying things like "Don't worry. This happens all the time. I have a sensitive stomach." And he wants to drive me home and I insist no. Finally the cab comes and he gives me the money for it.

And I'm going home and the sun is coming up and I start bleeding all over this cab, right? And I couldn't sleep. And I'm washing out my dress and around ten the phone rings and I know it's him. It rang like fifty times. It was still ringing when I left the apartment. Poor guy.

***

Published in "Urban Myths" by NuAge Editions.

Waiting for the Parade

John Murrell

Five women in Calgary work for the war effort in the 1940s, while their husbands are overseas. Tragedy and humour mingle as each of them copes with the effects of a long war on their daily lives.

JANET stands and smiles, speaking to the audience as though addressing a small, informal gathering.

JANET

I shook hands with them. Yes, both of them. That's when it really started for me. May 26, 1939. Of course, war hadn't been declared yet — wouldn't be declared for months. But some of us knew what was coming. We knew the significance of a Royal Visit at such a time. And it was when I shook hands with them that I understood the supreme sacrifices that would be demanded of each of us. The Queen even spoke to me. She has the loveliest complexion. She said, "The weather's very pleasant, isn't it?" I told her, "We always have a splendid May and June in Alberta. And July." And while I chatted with Her Majesty, I said to myself 'Yes. Yes, we're still children of this great Empire. Though thousands of miles of sea and land may divide us. We have traditions and beliefs we'd be willing to die for. Even here in Canada!' If I had a brother or a son I'd be proud to see him go! I'd sing and I'd cheer and I'd wave from the platform as his train disappeared into the night! (*slight pause*) My husband wanted to go. Desperately. But he's part of an "essential service." He reads the Texaco News Flashes, afternoons and evenings. And let me tell you, the miracle of radio is one thing that holds this country together today. (*pause*)

She smiles, takes a slip of paper from her pocket and reads.

"The next meeting of the Red Triangle will be held this Tuesday at four in Room 6 of the YWCA. Subjects to be discussed include 'Welcome to Calgary' handkerchiefs for our newly-arrived New Zealanders. Also, contrary to rumour, the scrap collection will continue until further notice." (*a big smile*) Thank you.

***

Published by Talonbooks.

Cake-walk

Colleen Curran

Five unlikely contestants clash in a cake-baking contest on Canada Day during which each contestant gets his or her just desserts.

RUBY

It's parade music and it's the only kind that's worth anything. I know. I lead parades in this town, right down MacKenzie King Street for Santa Claus. Three years running. I was the North Pole Head Fairy with my magic baton. But then it stopped. So did I. Because I broke my heart. I lost it, the thrill of the twirl. I came this close to being on "The Wayne and Shuster Show." What's so funny about Wayne and Shuster? But I didn't get on.

Because of Corey Jo Cronyn. Only everyone called her Lucy. Because she was so funny, like Lucille Ball you know? A week before my mother was going to drive me into Toronto to audition at the CBC, there was a Variety Show at the high school. Now I was really looked up to there because of my baton twirling. There was gonna be a tribute in my honour at the show. I sat there with my sisters Opal and Pearl and all my family and relatives. The band starts playing my Sousa music...the curtains open and there's Corey Jo in my costume and she's twirling an invisible baton. And she does all my routines only she does them all wrong and the crowd is laughing and everyone pointing at me with tears of laughter running down their faces. And it just broke my heart. The English teacher said it was flattery for someone to do impressions of you. But I didn't believe her. About the same time Buckeye started working at the Sunoco Station and he came by in his new uniform and he looked so good in it. He said he had a job and could support me and would be honoured to marry a star such as me.

I invited Corey Jo to the wedding and she cried all through the ceremony and then went and did her impression of me at the reception. And to this very day my Coral and Jade have never been told that their Mama was a Twirler Extraordinaire.

***

Published by Playwrights Canada Press in "Four New Comedies".

Into

Dave Carley

*The Urban Nun. She is dressed in a modern habit, probably
modified for the summer, identifiable and urban. She might have
sunglasses. She smokes with abiding pleasure.*

NUN

I'm an urban nun;
I take my God with smoke.
I take him loud. Rumbling like the Queen car.
Howling drunk. Crazy with despair
A thorn in the side. A kick in the gut
Don't want him leafy gold leafy, green leafy, palm leafy.
Don't want him pastoral. Pastoral is death.
And yeah, yeah, death is a comfort.
But comfort is false.

(*a letter appears magically*)

So this comes.
An invitation. To an up-north, get-down Nunfest.
A Retreat for all the remaindered nuns of the world.
The valiant last two hundred.
All of us called to a fine and quiet place of birds and bugs and birds and
bugs. And bugs.
So many, many bugs.

(*long, disgusted sigh*) Nuns alfresco.

(*reading*) "In God's own perfect nature."

I think not. If nature's so perfect God won't be there.
What's for him to do? Relax? God's going to relax?
Maybe he's going to lie under a tree and daydream new plagues?
Right.

She remembers the letter and shrugs.

But I go. If only to remember what my sisters look like.
Hey — even nuns get nostalgic! We get lonely! I get lonely!
I'll often dig out my convent yearbook on a slow Saturday night and
  imagine proms that never were, football games never cheered. Clash
  Days that faded into black and white.
I'll recall novices who slipped on the trip up God's altar.
And I'll curse the sisters who never visit me because of the trough of
  incorrectness in which I wallow.

We retreat by bus and car minivan multivan, mountain bike.
Some hobble barefoot up the northern concessions —
Barefoot Nuns of Perpetual Atonement — grateful for the gravel, the
  sharper the better.
And, arriving by float plane? You guessed it — the Yankee Techno
  Nuns.
We're met by Sister Katherine. Kate the Innocent.
My bunkmate way back when.
A vestal goofball sap with a Saran Wrap smile.
Kate welcomes us to the lodge, her arms upraised like a Rio statue.

For just a second she raises her arms.

Naturally there's an orientation cocktail party.
and yes, the jokes are just what you'd expect from a giggle of
Godbrides:
Requests for Virgin Marys. Purple Jesuses. Rusty Nails.
but funny thing — the walls of isolation begin tumbling like Jericho.
We're so diverse, this last two hundred. We're so international, We're so
  intercultural. Yet we're also interlinked by this umbilical wince of
  faith.
A tender bond fortified with booze.
So: when Kate gets out her Singing Nun guitar? And warbles
  Kumbayeh? Like a Kate Bush with hymen?
Well: shut up. Show some respect.
A musical cliché chased with Scotch can cure any sister's blues.
And: when someone suggests a little splish-splash?
Don't even think about laughing.
God's tilted the world into darkness.

His moon is warming the lake.
His sand fleas are urging us off the beach.
So we strip! And we run!
Carmelites, Ursulines, Josephines, Magdalenes. Militants, Pacifists,
Militant-Pacifists. New Agers, Mainliners, Hardliners, One Liners.
The chaste and the chased!
The dogmatic, the pragmatic, the stigmatic!
The night is filled with the rustling of shedding habits!
Falling wimples muffling fleabeach
Twittering like a hundred plucked ravens we pound over naked sand.
An army of motoring legs and arms.
We immerse in the northern waters!
Two hundred throats — gasp! Four hundred nipples — pop!
It's a glory of dunking sisters! A nubile of nuntits!
Nuntits, nunarms, nunbushes!
Dark sacred nunbushes!
Oh, baby baby!
I float out on my back, past them all.
I look up at the moon and the stars
Stars that might spell God if anyone could remember the language —
And I say, "Things don't get much better than this."
Exactly.
They start getting worse.

***

Published by Playwrights Canada Press in "Taking Liberties & Into".

Sanctuary

Emil Sher

Every week, June — an emotionally abused woman — retreats to a secluded spot in a park for some time alone. For a year, Philip has watched her from a distance. He introduces himself on the very morning when June has come to scatter her husband's ashes. June asks Philip if he has ever seen anyone burn, then recounts the memory of a childhood doll.

JUNE

Betty. Her name was Betty. Betty with the beautiful eyes. Blue, blue, blue. Long, dark lashes. Soft, blond hair. Didn't weigh more than a pound. (*pause*) My absolute favourite doll. Barbie was too bony. Her tits scared me. And I never trusted Ken. Too perfect. But Betty was mine. (*pause*) I can't remember exactly what it was I'd done, but I'd done something to make my mother angry. Really angry. She must've been having a hard day. Yeah, I'm sure she was just having one of those days. I was about five, maybe six. I probably did what every five-year-old does at one time or another, something that makes a parent's eyes turn funny. I said I was sorry. But that wasn't good enough. That's not good enough, young lady. My mother must have told me that a thousand times. Do you know what happens to young girls who misbehave? That's when she did it. I begged her not to, but she wouldn't have any of it. She plops Betty onto a tray and throws her into the oven. Soon there's this awful smell filling the kitchen. I stood there, practically blind for all the tears in my eyes. My mother walks in every ten minutes to check on Betty. "Look, June. Look what's happening to Betty." And she made me look, making me promise I'd always behave. Betty's arms and legs were melting, melting and her hair was sizzling. On it went, 'til there was nothing left but a puddle of Betty, and two blue eyes.

***

Available as a copyscript.

Crossing the Line

Colleen Craig

*Set in the 1980s, in the backyard of a communal house in a white
suburb of Johannesburg, the play examines the lives of a group of
women caught in the web of South African politics. Paula, a white
activist in her mid-twenties, has been sublimating her repressed
lesbianism through intense political activity and obsessive sexual
encounters with men. Here, Paula tries, for the first time, to speak
to Rosie, the woman she is deeply attracted to, about her feelings.*

PAULA

Understand? To analyze. Admit up to things. To talk about oneself is
not understanding!

I've been watching you too. You go on about feelings as if it were
nothing. Going around hugging everyone in that way you have.
Spontaneous! Sorted out! Cool!

We're not all like you!

You haven't had people tell you all your life that you're clumsy and
awkward and angry. That you don't fit in. You're too loud. Or too quiet.
A difficult phase. A difficult child. Blamed for things you didn't do. A
glass chipped. An ornament broken. It must be Paula! So one quiet
Sunday you go and smash the whole fucking row of them — to
smithereens — just to know that you really did do it!

Rules! Codes! Regulations! All set up according to their logic. No one
questions it. No one seems to feel a thing. Only you and nothing fits.
So by day you pretend to play their pretty smiling games, but at night,
alone, there is only you. Sometimes I lie there and it feels like it's all
pressing down on me. All that fear and confusion...here. There is no
mercy only darkness, around me, and in me. The next day the feeling is
still there but you don't let it show. That's surviving. And anger
becomes your armour. Your life swells out of control...sleeping with

guys, you can't remember how it began. Something to do with that darkness at night...believing the things they said, needing to hear... desperately needing to hear those things...(*her voice breaks*) From one to another to another...all the while...How do you expect me to handle this. I've been through this before. With Sarah. All these churnings, and no name for what I was feeling. So I try to work it out. On my own. This is something, I tell myself. On my own I figure out this is something — these feelings are real! Nothing from her side. Just my own messy, confused needs and who to talk to?

How can you do that! Out of the blue you announce that you're going to leave. Not that I didn't know it was coming. I did! I just thought that maybe...I mean...after all the warmth, the care you took, those things you said, how special I was...and then out of the blue. Not a word — I thought it was all inside my head.

No! You're leaving anyway. Just go then. (*a soft plea*) Go! Please!

***

Available as a copyscript.

Rosie Learns French

Carol Bolt

*Technically not a monologue, this piece involves a young
woman talking on the telephone to a man she is still in love
with but who does not feel the same way.*

ROSIE

Hello, operator...I'm calling this number collect...j'aimerais appel a cet
number collect...Cinq. Cinq. Cinq. Un. Deux. Froid. Six.

What? I mean quoi? Oh, shit, I mean, merde. Non je me regrette, cinq,
cinq, cinq, un, deux, trois, six. Je suis Rosie, dit "c'est Rosie qui appel."

Hello...allo, Rog?

C'est moi...Rosie...I don't know, I just wanted to call you. I missed
you. Because it's St. Jean Baptiste Day weekend and all I've got on are
my French Language Lesson Tapes. Premiere Leçon. First Lesson.
How are you? Ça va bien?

What do you mean?

What do you mean, "How come I'm home?" How come you're home?
At two a.m. on Friday night? How come you're not working? Is it all
those songs about animal rights or what? Is it Rejeanne?

I'm home because I got a new gig, Rog. In dinner theatre. It's a kind of
supper club. I do a show at nine. I do a show at eleven. (*she is aware he
knows that she's lying*) Dinner's at eight, Rog. What do you think, I'm
in Smith Falls? I'm in Edmonton, Rog...

Well, okay I'm not working tonight. I'm not working in some dumb
supper club. I'm working afternoons...

Pals.

It's a lounge, Rog.

Well, okay, it's a bar. I'm singing in a bar. In a motel on Stony Plain Road. In Edmonton.

All right, I'm not singing, but I'm working on a new act. It's a magic act. I get all dressed up, I put a diamond in my navel. I make things disappear.

I have this rabbit, this white rabbit, his name is Morris, he's right here, Rog. You want to say "Hello" to him? Say "Hello", Morris. Dites "Bonjour". (*to Roger*) He's bilangue.

I know you can't hear him, Rog, he doesn't talk. You think you have to talk to be bilingual? I'll bet there are thousands of people out there and you think they can't speak French, but that's just because they don't talk, Rog.

Because rabbits are mute, Rog, unless they're in pain. You want me to pull his ears? Just to prove I have a job and a bilingual rabbit?

I'm not depressed.

What makes you think I sound depressed?

I don't sound suicidal. Why would you think that I sound suicidal?

Oh, you remembered, eh? Last St. Jean Baptiste weekend.

And we had a picnic. In the park there, across from Jeanne Mance. And you said you were going back to school...

And everybody playing drums all day. (*she goes a little crazy*) Slam bam. Thank you, ma'am. Slam bam, thank you, ma'am. Slam bam thank you ma'am slam bam thank you ma'am...(*she continues until she drops the phone and dives for it, not wanting to lose contact*)

Rog, please, we were all dropping pills. I just dropped the wrong pills.

I'm not depressed. Please. I just miss Montreal, that's all. I miss you.

Don't say that, Rog.
It isn't over. I don't think it's over. Okay, you're there, I'm here, but that doesn't mean it's over, it doesn't have to be over.

What do you mean?

What do you mean, "It was over before." Before what?

I know we're friends, Rog. We're more than friends, Rog.

Please...don't say that. Don't say, "Je t'aime," like that. Don't sound like you're sorry.

Rog, I'm not sorry. I don't think it's over. And I get some say, don't I? I mean, you said, "Je t'aime." And you said we were friends. I mean, you can't just walk away, not if I'm hanging on your ankle.

Rog, don't hang up, okay?

Don't say that.

Don't say that. Don't sound like you're sorry, you bastard, you're not sorry.

Don't patronize me. Don't treat me like I'm in your Twelve-step Program.

Oh...no...please...

Don't worry about me, Rog. Please don't think I'm going to kill myself because you say, "Je t'aime, mais..." "Je t'aime mais c'est finis."

Mange la mard, Rog. (*she hangs up*)

Oh, shit. (*she picks up the receiver and punches "0" hurriedly*)

Hello, operator...I'm calling this number collect...j'aimerais appel a cet number collect...Cinq. Cinq. Cinq. Un. Deux. Froid. Six...C'est n'est pas occupé...It isn't busy. Try again, operator. Si'l vous plait, essayez une fois encore. C'est important.

***

Available from the author - contact Playwrights Union of Canada.

Dying to be Thin

Linda A. Carson

A look behind locked doors into the secret life of a young teenager battling the eating disorder bulimia, written from the author's personal experience.

AMANDA

(*pulling out a cooler*) Ice cream is great because I love it and it slides up super easily. (*taking a spoonful, savouring it and thinking*) You know how I first learned how to do this? I was only in Grade Five and my teacher, Miss Anderson, was giving us our first class in sex education. Well, I suddenly realized that I had never actually seen what a naked guy even looked like, so I went searching in the school library. I decided to try the medical section hoping a book would have a picture or something. Well, this huge yoga book caught my eye because it had this almost naked man on it's cover, wearing only this little diaper thing, doing all these contortions. I was looking through, hoping I could catch a glimpse up his loin cloth when I came to this chapter on cleansing. Here he was sitting cross-legged and he had a string going up one nostril and down the other and he was pulling it through to clean his nose! On the next page he had his stomach sucked in to about an inch wide and a little stream of water was pouring out of his mouth! It was called, "Cleansing the Stomach," and it said: "Drink five glasses of warm salt water, blow out all your air, suck your stomach in, and let the water pour out — or, if you must, give a small tickle at the back of the throat with your middle and index finger." Right away this idea popped into my head. I had just found out how fattening ice cream was, so, that weekend, I collected my allowance, hopped on my bicycle and beetled down to the Dairy Queen. And I bought myself this huge, loaded banana split. I sat right down there on the curb and I gobbled it in, mouthful after delicious mouthful. Then, I got back on my bike and cycled home. Mom and Dad were working and my sister was out so I locked all the doors. I went into the kitchen and I took down a big beer mug. I filled it with warm water and dumped in tons of salt, then I plugged my nose and glugged it all down. I did it again and again until I had five of them in my stomach.

Then I slowly made my way to the bathroom, put the toilet seat up, blew out all my air and pumped in my stomach — nothing happened. So I was about to put my fingers up toward my mouth when there was this huge explosion. Warm salty milky water came blasting out of my mouth. And it didn't go into a nice little stream — it went everywhere! All over floor, into the bathtub, up and over all the walls. and it kept coming — and it kept coming! And it went up and through my nose — and a piece of pineapple got stuck there — and there were bits of strawberries and blueberries and breakfast and — Yuk! I thought it was the grossest thing in all the world! I stopped. And I cleaned it all up, and I thought that I would never, *ever* do that again!

(*pause*) And I never did. Not once! I didn't even think about it again— (*forcing herself to face the truth*) — until I turned fifteen. Fifteen! I hated fifteen. I was perfect at fourteen. That's when this picture was taken. (*fishing out a photo*) But at fifteen I suddenly started to gain weight.

***

Published by Scirocco Drama.

Supreme Dream

Frank Moher and Rhonda Trodd

The true story of a young white woman from Calgary who toured as a "Supreme" exposes the underside of American showbiz, black/white relations, and cheap Holiday Inns.

RHONDA

One thing I notice is the guys in the band head right back to their cabins after rehearsal, and just stay there until it's time for the show. And these cabins are more like cells than rooms. I talk to Jerome the drummer about it, and he just says: "I'm a night owl," and tells me he's fine. I talk to Horace about it, but Horace just says to me: "Rhonda. Look around." We're sitting in a corner booth after the show — they'll only sit in a corner booth — and Horace says to me: "What don't you see here? Other than this table, what don't you see?" And I get it. finally, I get it. and Horace says to me, "If we went onto the shuffleboard deck, the shuffleboard deck would clear. If we went into the dining-room at lunch, after about half an hour there'd be a circle of empty tables all around us. Mary is protected, because Mary is a star. But we're not stars. And it may be fun to have the swimming pool to yourself the first couple of times, but after that...it isn't fun anymore."

And I tell him that's ridiculous. Yes, I, in my simple wisdom, tell him they're all wrong, it's not that bad, and somehow I convince them to come with me when we dock the next day — we're going to dock for the day at this private resort on the gulf Coast, we can go into town, go shopping, have lunch, *c'mon* you guys, I tell them, I need company. So they come. And Horace's little boy, who has arrived from Detroit to spend a week with his Dad, comes too.

Around three in the afternoon, Horace and his son and I end up playing Frisbee on the private beach. Now I can see the looks we're getting from the guests on the beach, and I realize, they think we're married, they think Horace and I are married and Horace's son is our kid, and oh oh isn't it shocking. And Horace is right — this little circle does open up around us, for about fifteen yards all around us, this little circle of very white sand, and there we are, Horace and me and Horace's son, playing Frisbee in the centre of it. Until the security guard arrives. He won't even look at Horace, just comes up to me and asks if we're staying at the hotel and I say no no we're staying at that fifty million dollar cruise ship over there, and maybe he'd like to check that out with my boss, Mary Wilson, of The Supremes. And he just says, "Maybe it would be better if you went back there, now." And I look at Horace, and I look at Horace's son, who's looking up at his Dad to see what his Dad's going to say. And Horace just says, "Let's go," and he starts back toward the ship.

That night, I went to apologize to Horace. He said, "Forget it. I knew what was going to happen. I just wanted you to see.

"I guess it's different up where you live, huh," he said to me. And I just stood there. What could I say? That the Metis kids in my neighbourhood might not think so? That up in Canada no one would ever throw him off a beach — not in February, at least. So I didn't say anything. but what I thought was — the world is really screwed."

***

Available from the author - contact Playwrights Union of Canada.

Path With No Moccasins

Shirley Cheechoo

*A one-woman show based on the author's personal experiences
in residential schools that reveals astounding truths about the
abuses suffered by many Native children in their formative
years.*

SHIRLEY

My cousin farted in class yesterday. She was so cute going (simulating
the sound) until she saw Miss Stapleton walking over. The teacher
grabbed her by the hair and pulled her to the front of the class. 'What do
you say?' Silence. Jessie was searching for an answer from us. We
didn't know what she was supposed to say. Teacher kept yelling, "What
do you say useless dirty girl? What do you say you stupid Indian girl?"
Jessie's eyes lit up. Ours did too. She found what to say. She looked so
brave. She stood up straight and said "Oops."

Miss Stapleton, who is she to do that? She has bad breath that stinks
worse than the dogs on the reserve. She spits in our faces, even when
she just talks. She chews cigarettes you know. Her teeth are all brown
and crooked and they stick out from everywhere. Reminds me of a dog's
mouth, the mouths that almost killed me once, those husky dogs that
ripped at my clothes trying to eat my blood. They wanted something
inside me. I think she's one of them dogs. She punished Jessie for her
smell but who's gonna punish that teacher for her smell? It won't be the
principal. She has something over him I think.

***

Published as a trade paperback.

The Trial of Judith K.

Sally Clark

Roughly based on "The Trial" by Franz Kafka, this black comedy changes the lead character to a modern business woman who finds herself accused of an unknown crime. The more she delves into the bureaucratic nightmare the more her ordered little world unravels and the more she is entangled in the increasingly obscure and deadly process.

JUDITH

Calm down, Judith. This is not serious. That man-woman-man is not a government agent. He-she-whatever is simply Milly Pearce watching the soap opera. (frantic) Yes, but where's Mrs. Block! (calmly) Edna has merely over-reacted. It is up to you, Judith, to straighten things out. You are going to get organized. You show up on Sunday. (frantic) Yes, but what time! They never gave me a time. (calmly) Early, Judith. You get up bright and early. Make the long trek out to Surrey. (frantic) God! I wish I had a car. (reasonably) You don't have a car, Judith. You will take the bus, instead. (frantic) The bus! That'll take forever. And what will I do when I get there! What will I say!

You're going to be aggressive, Judith. Polite, but aggressive. Assume they've made a mistake. Make a joke of it. (laughing in a sophisticated manner) Be understanding. After all, it's not their fault they're stupid. Most people are stupid. They don't organize their lives. You are going to be prepared.

RIGHT!

YEAH OKAY RIGHT!

GET ORGANIZED!

***

Published by Playwrights Canada Press.

The End

John Palmer

Curry is between 25 and 35. Her hair is a mess but her make-up is perfect. She's having morning coffee with two other women. She wears a bracelet made of Cracker-Jack prizes, in the play about the decline of Western civilization mirrored in an assembly of bizarre characters all suffering from identity crises.

CURRY

Sheez. I always wondered why I couldn't get along with women. 'Cause they're crazy. Webster and me had a couple of laughs. Ha ha finished. He thought I was funny. You get out there honey and play ball. You got a good thing going. Webster's a nice guy. Basically screwed up but nice. See now I only do it with guys I'm nuts about. I used to do it with anybody. Hell, all right, I used to be a tart. In order to be a successful tart, I had to be pretty good in bed. I decided on a systematic approach. I worked Carlton Street for six months, only with young guys who were lousy at it, they didn't care what was happening, it's just that it was actually happening for real, so they got it off fast. I learned like hell. Then I moved to The Plaza. Hit the mid-thirties set, the ones with the three-year itch. They paid better. Almost drove me crazy tellin' me how great their wives were: guilt. Like every one of them personally nailed Jesus. After a year, I knew I was ready for the big time. I got a real flashy apartment — had it done up fantastic — twenty-five fags runnin' around in circles. Men from forty-five to sixty-five are it. They know how. They know what. They got money. No guilt. No hang-ups. Lonely, horny men who know the score. So I made lots of money but I really screwed up my head 'cause it started to feel empty after. All those lonely guys. I knew I was crackin' up. I said to myself, "Curry, what do you need this for?" I stopped being a tart. That was the beginning of the end. I kept falling in love with one wonderful guy after another. It was perfect. Oh yeah. I was in love. Sex was wonderful. He was wonderful. I said to myself, "Curry, what the hell's coming off?" I was the loneliest person in the world. Justin didn't love me, he loved good ol', stupid ol' curry, the barrel o' laughs sexpot with the heart of gold. An' I was. So he was. Dumb. How many laughs do you get outta your average barrel. I made myself what I am and now I can't get out. Goddammit, I'm a person. She's not a bad person, though I never met her, but I know she's there. She doesn't collect Cracker-Jack prizes.

When she says funny things people laugh with her. Holy Jesus, she's a nice person. She knows how to love. He would love her. In his arms it would be quiet for a long time. No yukking it up. Judy Malone you may be a hulk but yer figgerin' it out. Dumb. Curry, rots a ruck.

***

Published by Coach House Press.

Cyber: womb

Vivienne Laxdal

Several years of failed attempts to conceive a child has ruined her marriage and pushed Oneida Kilborn over the edge. In this fantasy sequence, she undergoes a new fertilization procedure.

ONEIDA

I am given chemical relaxants. Doctor Krumm assures me that these chemicals are in no way harmful to me, or my soon-to-be-conceived babies. We have agreed upon twins, as we may not be able to do this more than once. My body and my mind must exist at the peak of susceptibility. I am conceptually susceptible.

I wait for the familiar drill, or the poke or the tweak of some none-too-distant painful procedure, but I feel nothing. They assure me it is not because I am frozen, but because this method is not such that requires the crude utensils of in-vitro fertilization gone past, but this is a cyber-system of embryo construction. One that is completely painless.

They ask me which sense-memory tape I would like to play, while they tend to the physical details. I chose "The Night of the Laughing Orgasm". What better way to split your first cell than inside a womb massaged by euphorically joyful contractions?

Unlike other orgasms, often accompanied by the uncontrollable release of sadness and tears, this night is different. As the sensation increases — that unmistakable assurance that all is well, and indeed this is going to be one of those rare, lucky times — a faint and funny tickling under the ribs coincides with my pelvic eruptions. I am overwhelmed with glee and burst into spontaneous laughter which is both surprising and confusing to Robert, but pleasing none the less.

The doctor removes the cyber-system devices of invirtual fertilization. The first phase of conception is complete. We must now await the verdict, of which I am certain, is this time, to be positive.

***

Available as a copyscript.

The Saints and Apostles

Raymond Storey

*Madeline is roommate to Michael, a professional director in his
30s who has fallen for a youth, barely out of his teens who is HIV
positive, and, eventually, dying. Madeline, while trying to support
Michael, is not happy herself, and has deep feelings for him.*

MADELINE

The summer of '75 was the summer of rage. That summer, my picture
was featured twice in *The Kitchener-Waterloo Record*. Once for being
the first girl — sorry, woman — ever to man the pumps at the DX Gas
Bar, and then later when I married Roddy Fountaine.

Photo One: Maddy Dixon wearing yellow, terry hot pants, sandals with
three-bloody-inch platform soles, and a DX Gas Bar T-shirt, two sizes
too tight. She is spread-eagle against a '71 Chevy Malibu with its hood
up — reaching for the dipstick.

Check out the eyes. You see, Maddy Dixon honestly thinks that she is
striking a blow for the sisterhood. She actually believes that being
Kitchener's first pumpwoman is newsworthy. But she is eighteen, and
she doesn't think she's pretty, and she's never met a real photographer,
and he just asked her to bend over a fender. And by the time he squats
behind her with his wide-angle lens, she is past the point of no return.
And in the snap of a shutter, Maddy Dixon's ass is a three-colour
spread. And for the rest of the summer, redneck jerks will lean out of
their half-tons, hollering, "Fill'er up, Maddy! And crack me a smile!"

Picture number two: Mrs. Roddy Fountaine. She is wearing white-
polyester-eyelet-lace with an empire waist, a princess neckline and
belled sleeves. That thing on her head is called a picture hat. God knows
why.
Don't look at the eyes. They say nothing.

You see, Mrs. Roddy Fountaine is eighteen years old and she still doesn't think she's pretty. But she's never been married. And her mother called it jitters, and the minister called it nerves, since she was way past the point of no return, and she couldn't tell them why.

'Cuz she was too afraid to say it, but last week when they went camping, and she and Roddy'd had a couple of beers, Roddy tried to shove a coke bottle up inside her — and she thinks he's going to kill her.

***

Published by Playwrights Canada Press.

Angelique

Lorena Gale

Marie Josephe Angelique, a slave in 18th century Montréal, has given birth to a child from an unwanted liaison with her master, François de Francheville. here, she talks to the child before taking its life.

ANGELIQUE

In the beginning there was darkness. Dense. Profound. Darkness. Like a thick black blanket stretching into seamless infinity. The darkness was all and all was darkness. Is and would ever be. And the darkness slumbered. Complete in her ebony world.

Til one day there was a movement. A stirring. A rumbling somewhere deep inside. An unacknowledged longing to be more than everything. Growing like the sound of distant thunder. Unsettling her dreams. But not enough to wake her.

The stirring grew into a churning. The darkness swirled and eddied. Rising and crashing in on herself. She rocked. She reeled. Until she woke. And then she knew that she would never sleep again.

'Something has changed in me. I can no longer bear to be alone.'

And with that thought the darkness heaved and pushed. Forcing desire from her depths. Giving birth to light. Light was small. No bigger than a spark. But in it, darkness could see the full extent of herself.

'I am so much more than what I thought I was.'

And light blinked with the bright eyes of a newborn. Dazzling. Delighting the darkness. And a great heat she had never before noticed spread through darkness as she closed protectively 'round light. Like a mother cradling her child.

Light, unlike darkness, came into being complete with its own self-knowledge — which it fed on with a ferocious hunger. Growing fatter. And pushing back the darkness in defiance. The darkness, being everywhere, still encompassed the light no matter how she strained to give it room.

The light, fueled by its own existence, grew hotter in confinement.

'I am so much more than what I am. At least as much as darkness — which is everywhere. Why must I be contained? Without me, the darkness has no knowledge of itself. Therefore I am everything. And the darkness is nothing.'

The light burned with greater arrogance. Growing hotter and denser with a simmering anger, which bubbled and popped beneath its surface of brilliance. And still the darkness closed around it.

'I am more than...I am more than this...I am more than this,' it seethed. Till it was so full of itself that it exploded, sending shards of its being hurling through the darkness and lighting up the void.

The light was now everywhere. Cutting through the darkness with the sharpness of an ax. Cruelly severing the umbilicus between them. the darkness was so blinded by the light that she could no longer see. And so retreated to where she could have some sense of herself. Though light still pierced her — as a reminder that it now ruled everything.

Light and darkness.

That is how the two became separate forces. In constant opposition. Light in the forefront. And darkness. Waiting on the edge of everything.

When the first white man came to our village, he was no surprise to us. Because we had observed light and dark play itself out in everything around us. Even you, my baby. Where light and dark have clashed and come together. When we saw those white faces, we knew the explosion had come and the long period of waiting had begun. And so we walked towards our destiny. Our heads held high. Our eyes wide open.

But there is something else we know, my child. that in the end...the darkness reclaims everything. The stars will fall. The sun will cease to shine. Light will collapse in on itself. Til once again, it is nothing more than just a little spark. That flickers, sputters, pops itself out. The darkness will resume her peaceful reign.

***

Available from the author - contact Playwrights Union of Canada.

No More Medea

Deborah Porter

The Virgin Mary and Medea find themselves on Bloor Street trying to determine if much has changed in a millennium or two - besides shopping and the burden of mythological figures.

MEDEA

So.
Now we see what strong, true men are made of.
When going to the market, it's easy to tell
The good fruit from the soft and overripe:
But men are different things,
And many a fine exterior hides a weak and shameless heart.
Still, I suppose the fault is mine, for succumbing to
The bittersweet pain that is called love.
Never mind that now. What's done is done.
Besides, I'm "entertaining" the loveliest idea for revenge.
I'll call Jason back, and speak so soft
That he cannot refuse my small request. It goes like this:
"I've had a change of heart. Good luck, and I go willingly,
But let the children stay. They are too young to live
In that arid plain where I must be content."
I hate to use the kids as chattel in this battle;
But, I need them to fulfill my plan.
He will agree.
I'll send them to the palace with gifts for the bride:
A dress of silk, and coronet of gold,
Which I'll prepare and fill with the deadliest poison known
to man.
She'll gasp with pleasure, put them on —
And burn to death with most exquisite pain.
Any that touch her will also die, so potent is this venom!
And thus is made my vengeance on her and that oafish king.
Jason will be upset too, I know,
But I have further plans to deal with that traitor.

And surely now my mother's heart must shrivel up and die.
I'll kill the children.
Oh, Medea, what is wrong with you
That such a plan was ever born?
Your gentle babes! Their silken hair and rosy cheeks — stop!
But I see no other way.
They go with me — they die.
They stay — they'll die for sure.
My murder of the boys will save them from crueler hands,
And is the surest way to torture Jason.
Oh gods!
I won't be scorned or mocked as a spurned thing
I am of royal blood myself, grand-daughter of Apollo.
Many women take this kind of treatment as their due
And are forced to, in a world that hates our sex.

I am a different creature, and will not!
Oh yes — I'm foul, I am the vilest of women,
The nursing bitch who thwarts the trust of her pup.
Now, History: Come. Plot my course.
I'll be the monster for your books and plays
So be it. Seal my fate.

***

*Published by Playwrights Canada Press
in "Flowers & No More Medea".*

The Obeah Man

Richardo Keens-Douglas

*Dora is a landlady who befriends Joshua, a black man living in
her building. Life has been tough on him because of his
colour, so he calls up the Obeah Man (magic man) from the
islands to come and make everything right. The Obeah Man
arrives, and not only changes Joshua's life but also Dora's.
Here she tells Joshua about her wedding, something she has
never spoken about since she was stood up, but the Obeah
Man gave her the strength to talk about her past.*

DORA

I don't know. Since he's been here, I've been thinking. Thoughts I never
thought about before. I don't know if it's his doing or what. Did you
know I hated it when it rained? But since I've met you I have come to
love stormy nights. We always seem to have the most fun on nights
like these. You just make them seem so magical. You know why I
hated the rain? Because it never rained on my wedding day. Joshy I had
the most beautiful day any bride could ever dream for. The sun found
every open crack in that little church and just beamed down on
everyone. Like little spotlights. It was as if the rays were tickling
them. They all had these smiles on their faces. But he never showed. I
was dressed to the nines. My train was so long and heavy, it looked like
I was ready to do a back flip. My dress...my dress...was so beautiful.
We couldn't have dreamed it up any better. Fit for a princess. Two
hours...I waited. Alone. Imagine that, all dressed up and no place to go.
The thoughts that ran through my head about that man would put our
little games to shame. You know what was nice though? They all
waited with me. Not one person left. Even the little flower girl. That's
what I miss. Children. Then I looked to the back of the church and there
was a figure standing in the doorway. But I couldn't see who it
was...the glare. It...it...looked so much like him. I started to walk
towards the light...very fast...and...he vanished. He was there. I know
he was. And I stood in the middle of that aisle, and I just wanted it to

rain and spoil everything. Because it was turning out to be the ugliest moment of my life, yet the day was so beautiful. At least if it had rained, I could have said it was a lousy day to get married on anyway.

***

Available from author - contact Playwrights Union of Canada.

Scary Stories

Gordon Armstrong

*From the "Feeding William" section of the play. The speaker,
Midge, is a housewife in a U.S. suburb of the 1950s. She has just
discovered her next-door neighbour, Bill, bound to a chair in his
blood-splattered kitchen; she immediately falls into a private
reality.*

MIDGE

Where is my son? I'm looking for my son. We haven't seen him since
last night — he ran out after supper, it was very strange, at first I
thought he was just going out in the yard, but later I thought — the
way he ran out, it was like he was eager, meeting someone, desperate to
see someone. I've never felt that from him before. He's only fourteen,
he's not even the age when I started to be afraid of boys — he's still a
bit of a stick in his gym-strip, face still shines like a doll's. Is it
starting younger, the wilderness that grows in boys? That sullenness.
Like the child has finally found something to hate, something worth
hating. If he's gone somewhere — well, it's impossible to know, not
with Freddy, what secrets he's scouting out. Jim's out looking, driving
around the parts of town we were so careful to never tell him about. Is
he there? Does he know there's a dark, low path, a way to see the
secrets in gaudy detail, and peel them away like leaves off an artichoke?
The secrets of boys. I can't name them. I just want to find my son, so
I'm looking—

What I have found. What I have found is an abyss deeper than the sweet
shallow nothings of airtight cathode-lit living rooms. A pit with walls
of flesh, the raw carcass of hope. I've heard the crack that little lives
make when they break, and seen sights that would make God himself
recoil...and dark figures like frightened animals, crouched low,
trembling, clinging to deluded dreams of — possession — I have this. I
have the feasts of hell.

***

Available as a copyscript.

Miracle Mother

Deborah Kimmett

This mordant comedy looks at both the experience of delivering a very premature baby as well as the entire birth experience reflected in the mother-daughter relationship.

MARY

My mom would never hug me. It used to drive me nuts. I even went back East a couple of weeks before she died, determined that I was going to get her to hug me, come hell or high water. I sat there the first night, waiting for her, trying to will her into it. To drown her in "white light and God's love", but she sat there with that wretched face of hers, bent over a china cup, dunking biscuits into Red Rose tea, while she second-guessed the answers on Jeopardy. After about three nights of this I couldn't take it any longer. I walked over and grabbed her and hugged her so hard she almost had an infarction. The tea cup flew out of her hand and spilled all over the TV Guide and she roars, "What the hell are you doing, Doctor?" Even though I was her daughter, she always called me Doctor. Whenever we went out to a movie or a play she'd always yell, "Doctor, how much were the tickets?" Or "Doctor, are you going to pick up the popcorn?" I told her she was being prideful. She told me it was to let people know that if they got sick there was someone in the audience that could help them. I said, "I am going to give you a hug." She says, "Well, you should warn a person so they'll know it's coming." Then she put down her tea and sat their waiting like a drill sergeant with her arms locked by her side. "Go ahead, Doctor."

I hugged her so hard I almost strangled her. I hated her. I hugged her every night for two weeks and finally on the night before I was supposed to go home the miracle happened. I got up from my chair to hug her and she had her arms up first. (*pause*) I realized something. She didn't know how to hug me until I showed her how.

She died the next day.

It was the first time I let her off the hook.

***

Published by Scirocco Drama.

The Perfect Pie

Judith Thompson

Patsy is sending a tape-recorded letter and package to Marie, her best friend, who killed herself many years ago.

PATSY

My mum said for me to watch her meatpie, Marie. She counted on me, she instructed me to turn that oven off in sixty minutes' time, oh orange light, it is snowing outside, over the tulips out back, and the snowdrops, the fat flakes coming on down, we lie on the hook rug, the TV's on, just a laugh-track, we're eating chips, sour cream and onion, we're sharing a large bag, and we got the Tabs and we're just, like, talking, about nothing, about if we should get our hair cut short and how come I get cramps so bad on my period and you look at me and you say, "Patsy, I would rather die than have my life here, in Marmora," and I go, "Well Marie, you don't have to have your life here, my sister took off out west when she was sixteen and she's doing fine," and your face goes purple, I mean purple, and you look right at me in my eyes and you go, "Patsy, I do not have the heart. I do not have the heart to leave, I do not have the heart to stay." Then you're taking me by the hand, you take me out the back door and we're looking at the sun going down over the tracks and you whisper to me, "We'll be martyrs, Marmora martyrs," and I thought you were kidding, or talking like poetry in English class, but you keep on, "They will build a statue of us in the park," you say, "in stone," and I follow you up to the tracks and the snow keeps coming down, we're standing on the tracks in our running shoes with the snow all swirling round; my feet's getting freezing, I got no socks, and the light from the house and the orange, and the coppery smell of the pie burning; it's burning, oh my God my mother's pie! And then I hear the whistle, and I remember I forgot to take the pie out, and you squeeze my shoulder and you say, "See you after, Patsy, in the hand of God, " and then I seen it, coming, bigger and bigger the train so loud so black, screaming screaming, "There it is, right there right there." I try to pull you away, off the tracks, like, "Come on, Marie, Marie are you crazy, come on the train is coming, my mum's pie, I gotta get it out, the pie is gonna burn," alls I wanted in the whole world was to save that pie, I was gonna get in deep, my mum hated the way the smell of something burnt stayed in a house for so long, she hated it, and alls I could see was that pie turning black, I flew off that track.

You should have come with me; jump off the track, roll down the hill, hit the rocks, gash; you should have come with me.

There wasn't no statue, Marie. Just a article in the paper. And I'll be honest with you, I haven't heard anybody even mention what happened for, oh, I'd say ten years. So as far as Marmora goes, you are gone. You're gone. But as far as I go, well, I'll tell you, this is gonna sound mental, but some times when I make my pastry, I think I'm making you, kneading the dough till, till my hands they are aching and, and I, like, form you; right in front of my eyes, right here at my kitchen table, into flesh. Looking at me, talking soft.

Marie, along with this tape you will hopefully find one frozen steak and kidney pie. I just hope it don't break apart in the mail but if it does just shove it in the microwave, it'll taste just fine. If you ever need a break from the big city we'd just love it if you'd stop by for a visit. We've got a spare room now that the boys are gone and you would be more than welcome to stay overnight. Well, anyways, Marie, I'll let you go. Please do drop me a line, and I hope you don't mind my being so bold and all, sending you this letter by a tape. I hope that we will start up being in touch, you know, maybe just Christmas cards, or whatever, and please do enjoy the pie. Oh...your best friend, Patsy.

She reaches over and turns off the tape recorder.

***

Published in "Solo" by Coach House Press.

In the Lobster Capital of the World

Don Hannah

*A gay man, Edward returns to his New Brunswick home with his
very young lover in tow and this makes waves with family and
friends, including Pat, a female friend of long standing.*

PAT

I don't want you to touch me. Mark was kind to me, you know? He
was very, very — oh, how can I say that he was kind? Don't touch me!
Oh, I'm so mad! I'm so sick of myself for waiting for that shithead to
make a commitment. He told me his favourite poem was "Dover
Beach" and I knew I could wait forever. Wait, wait, wait. All I do is
goddamn wait! Wait for men to come along and then when they do all
they do is keep me waiting.

I wish to Christ I'd never met you! I was better off before you made me
fall in love with all that crap—"Dover Beach" and Matisse and goddamn
Elisabeth Schwarzkopf singing those four last frigging songs. Without
you I'd have left university and gone back to Rexton. Married some guy
and been happy as a clam. By now I'd have kids big enough to ride
snowmobiles. My sisters' lives aren't so terrible. They aren't terrible at
all. In fact, they look pretty goddamn good after you've just spent five
years waiting for a commitment from some clown who won 't make
one, who will never make one. And after the things I did for him. And
nothing you do will make yours last either!

I know you. You used to walk down to the wharf with me, remember?
Back before little Tootsie Pie even knew how to walk. Mr. Poetry, Mr.
The-Sea-Is-Calm-Tonight, The-Moon-Lies-Fair-Upon-The-Coast, Mr.
Fill-Their-Heads-with-Crap! Sure, you can knock him over for a few
more months, but you and that kid will not last!

***

Published by Playwrights Canada Press.

Plague Monkeys

Conni Massing

Pat, 36, is talking to her sister, Bev, about Pat's 14-year-old daughter, Meg.

PAT

Meg, take off those headphones. Meg! (*beat*) The iron maiden has decided she's going to blackmail us. She says she'll commit suicide if we don't let her go to this concert. (*beat*) Ask her what happened the last time she went to a concert. Just ask her. (*beat*) She thinks she should be able to do anything she wants because I'm addicted to nose spray. She can come at two in the morning with pupils the size of grapefruits because I have sinus trouble! I have sinus trouble! (*beat*) I'm sorry. I'm really sorry. Believe me, I know what I sound like. But since Christmas...first she dyed her hair. All of her hair. Then she started coming home with marks on her arms. Slashes and...burns. We played seven-up — they pretend to slit their wrists.

(*beat*) It's like drowning, Bev. Big waves crashing in over my head, one after another. I just get the sea water pumped out of my lungs and the school phones again. Soon as there's trouble, Dave disappears. Meg won't talk and I can't stop crying and now there's some boy skulking around the house like a coyote waiting to get into the hen house. His name's Mordred or Morwyn or some goddamn thing that means death in Welsh and I think they're having sex and I...just...don't...know. (*whispering*) I think she's pregnant.

(*beat*) Look, all these years and I've never even asked you to baby-sit for half and hour. Please. Just for one night. Rent a movie. Let her have a beer or something. Maybe she won't hit you over the head and steal your car. (*beat*) Bev...I've got to talk to Dave and I can't do anything with Meg stomping around. It's like prying at the base of an active volcano. I'm gonna kill her or she's gonna kill me or...please. (*beat*) She likes you.

***

Available from the author - contact Playwrights Union of Canada.

Aunt Hannah Meets Joe River

Laurie Fyffe

*On her first night out of the Royal Ottawa Sanitarium, Hannah
tries to make her sister Lucinda understand her life with Charlie.*

HANNAH

You never came. Not even at Christmas. I used to decorate at
Christmas. Oh, yes, Charlie insisted. And we had a big tree, oh, not
some dinky thing you stick on a table top, no sir, big one, covered in
drapes of that tinsel stuff, gobs of it. And tiny blinking lights — blink,
blink! Blink, blink! And ornaments made out of glass, those ones
shaped like tear drops with scenes painted right on them. And this huge
gold star with points so sharp it used to pick a hole in the stucco
ceiling. And I sprayed the windows too, that white guck — Merry
Christmas! And, I put out a red and green checkered table cloth on the
dining room table, red and green, red and green, everywhere you looked.
Then I stuck this big, fat Santa Claus candle right in the middle. Yes
sir, anywhere you could stick Christmas, I stuck it. And, talk about
holly! We had bushels of the stuff! Running along the window sill,
around the doors, and, oh, those air fresheners, mustn't forget those
damn things, cinnamon, pine, gingerbread...place stunk of Christmas.
Course, he wanted me to bake. Oh, yes, everything he'd tasted at
Mother's, Charlie said I could make better. No matter how much work.
No matter how futile. Rum balls. Shortbread. Cathedral windows! And
the fruitcake, hell, there was never enough fruitcake. Dark and chunky,
with and without dates, light and spongy, with and without
coconut...and it had to be cut up, cut up and waiting...waiting! While
we sat there, just the two of us! Alone. In front of the idiot box. Room
full of the stink of pine needles! Tree winking and blinking, and a pile
of sweet, sticky fruitcake!

(*pause*) But nobody came. Nobody. Who was there?

***

Available as a copyscript.

The Voyeur's Tea Party

Jennifer Martin

Rosemary was supposed to meet a friend for a walk. She injures herself and has to cancel — but her friend comes over for a visit and Rosemary's monologue confirms her suspicions.

ROSEMARY

It was wonderful walking with you last week. I hadn't done the seawall in — maybe five years — for as long as I've had kids, anyway. It was so nice to have the luxury of just walking and talking, no worries...

I didn't know about the cormorants. I have to admit I was a little frightened when I first saw them — I always worry that black birds are portents of disaster. Read too much Carlos Castenada when I was younger, I guess. And Siwash rock is surrounded by legends and stories, so seeing these huge dark birds on the rock scared me. A warning of danger, foreboding, something to fear.

After I fell, the kids came down the stairs. I was starting to come to and off in a fog I could hear Robin yelling, "You killed her. You killed my mother. I told them, "Daddy didn't touch me. I just fell down the stairs." But they didn't believe me. They were sobbing so hard they couldn't stop. And then I started to get frightened because Rob can't stand crying, he never cries. He thinks it's weak.

As we walked along the seawall together, I could hear birds calling and crying against the wind. And then we turned a corner, at the north-west point, and there was that sheer rock face, and you said, "Watch your head". I hadn't noticed the signs, "Watch for falling rocks". Suddenly the seawall seemed like a dangerous place to be. Strange how the mood changed, just as we turned the corner. The day had been so pleasant, sunny and hot, peaceful, and then we walked into shadow. I was afraid the birds would follow us.

I don't know what happens to Rob. He is so sweet and then all of a sudden he'll get in a rage and he doesn't know what he's doing. Somehow I got the strength to get up and take both of my children to the darkest corner of the basement. They were in their pyjamas.

So there we were, huddled together, in the basement, in the dark, wondering what kind of home we live in that we're afraid to cry and I could hear Rob coming down the stairs, slowly, trying to figure out what was going on with us. What happened to his falling wife.

Falling wife. Falling wife. Falling rocks. You told me how dangerous it was, and then you said that someone had wanted to put a fence up along the rock face to protect passersby from the falling rocks, but they hadn't been allowed to, because of the cormorant nests.

And then I saw that all along the rock face, in every nook and cranny, there were nests, and cormorants flying, fighting the wind. Fighting the wind, so they could get low enough to dive into the water and look for food. No wonder they cried so hard.

And as we watched, a bird gave way. A gust of wind caught it and smashed it against the rock face. We didn't notice where the cormorant fell. Maybe it wasn't really hurt. I just turned my head, it made me too sad to look.

***

Available as a copyscript.

White Weddings

Marie-Lynn Hammond

*A story of hidden family truths, three sisters, and their dying
mother who is obsessed with romantic love and perfect weddings.
Alex is the oldest sister and has so far been unable and, or,
unwilling to fulfill the dreams of marriage her mother has for her.*

ALEX

I know all about The Dream. Doesn't matter that I don't believe it
anymore. I want it. I want it so bad I can taste it. There's this man, see.
He's about my age, not conventionally handsome, but his face has
character. He works out, so he's got good pecs, a nice little bum...and
he's bright, and witty, and he's never ever voted Conservative. Or
Liberal. He's a college prof with tenure — but he's in Labour Studies,
so it's all right. He is of course dying to have a child and he's fully
prepared to divide the childcare fifty-fifty. His current housemate is
lesbian — actually lesbian and black — so he's had to confront his
latent homophobic and racist tendencies. For a while he saw a
psychotherapist — a feminist woman psychotherapist, so he's dealt
with all his negative feelings about his mother. In other words he's not
at all afraid of intimacy, but for some reason he's willing and able to
deal with someone who is. Like me. He's not a wimp though. His
hobby is white-water rafting, but he doesn't expect me to go with him,
thank God. And — oh yeah. He's read his roommate's "Joy of Lesbian
Sex" from cover to cover, so he's fabulous in bed. So when I meet —
other men, men with good politics and bad bodies, or men with good
bodies who voted Conservative — they can't compete with him. And he
gets closer all the time, I even know what he smells like now, I know
the shape of his fingernails, the way the hair curls at the nape of his
neck. He grows and grows inside me, crowding out the others, crowding
out everything possible. He's perfect, except for one slight flaw: he
doesn't exist.

***

Available as a copyscript.

Take Care of Me

Florence Gibson

Marsha is 30 to 35, a corporate executive. She is nine months pregnant, in a tailored business suit. Contractions come with increasing intensity. She rubs her belly.

MARSHA

As a child, I searched, really searched, for some female meaning, some deity beyond my mother and my Sunday-school teacher. Christianity. All those women weeping in perpetuity: I felt flawed by a fundamental happiness. In grade five, I learned about the Greeks. I bonded with Diana, Goddess of the Hunt. Oh I realize now she has nothing much to offer the woman of today besides maybe a religious affiliation with Ducks Unlimited — but then! — she ruled the forest and she ran faster than anybody and I loved her! But when I ran faster than anybody they all ran into the club house and put up a sign that said "No girls allowed". (*contraction*)

As a child, I remember beating my fists against my mother's soft baby-scarred belly and screaming, "How come you can't make them take that sign off?!" (*contraction*)

As a woman I now feel I have personally taken that sign off every door I have ever encountered. I feel that I have personally earned the right to compete in the arena of male experience, that I have worked, that I have learned, that I deserve to be— (*contraction stops her*)

There is no need for a separate female spiritual experience. I think we all work together just fine, and my experience is testament to that. As a woman about to have a child I think everything is fine, just fine. I think everything is going to be great. (*big contraction*) Oooooooohhhh.

***

Available as a copyscript.

Claudius

Ken Gass

In this retelling of the legend of the mad Danish Prince which was also the source for Shakespeare's "Hamlet", Gertrude, the prince's mother, is the driving force and the survivor.

GERTRUDE is talking to EMILIA.

GERTRUDE

Your hair is so long now. You haven't cut it since your husband died, am I right? Mmm. Perhaps we should braid it then, would you like that? I braided mine, for my wedding, my first wedding. To Theodore. Braids weren't fashionable then, but soon, all the women were doing it. Yes, I'll braid your hair, and afterwards you can braid mine, agreed? (*no response*)

Listen, not a sound. The halls and corridors are finally still. And life goes peacefully on. You see? Women should rule the world, I'm convinced of it. We may be as bloody as the men, but we don't make an art of it. Women are practical. We do what is necessary, and then, we get on with living. And that is exactly what we shall do here. I've given instructions to the court to feed the poor, and clothe the naked children, Claudius never even cared about such things. See the collective good our tragedies have wrought! (*bursting out with laughter*)

Now shall you marry Laertes or shall I? I think you'd better, Emilia. No, I insist. His thighs are very firm, and he has a wonderful chin. With a short beard he'd look...dangerous, which would make my position...also dangerous. Yes, I think it'll be safer, much safer, if I remain celibate. At least for a while.

I'm not so young any more, am I? Yet I need passion. Claudius was a lion, a passionate brute, though he could've been a poet, he had the sensitivity, but politics interfered. It always does. I'll have to marry a solid man, ordinary perhaps, even boring, one whom I can control. How to find passion and safety in the same net, well, that's a problem for another age. Isn't it?

***

Published by Playwrights Canada Press.

Crazy Luv

Karen Kemlo

Margie Mullins is in her early 50s. She is talking to a cop about a con man who stole her money and her heart.

MARGIE

Well, when Walter died, everyone kept saying that I should wait one whole year to decide anything. Well, when it finally got close to the one year anniversary, I started going out. Just to a few parties, couple of dances. Oh, I know people were talking about me at church. I could hear them whispering. About the parties and how I'd started dying my hair. That was quite the scandal! Then one day, in the beauty parlour, I was reading my horoscope, and it said: "A change of life is coming your way, romance and travel are highlighted."

Well, so I took that as a sign, because right away I started feeling anxious, and my stomach was so tied up in knots I could hardly eat. I nearly didn't go to church. But I knew that if I didn't all the old biddies would be clucking and carrying on so loudly I'd never be able to show my face in town again. So I went. Now I know it was my destiny. Because as soon as I walked into that church my heart turned over. He was sitting in my pew!

Holding my hymn book. And the feeling I got when our eyes met, well...and all I could think about was how good looking he was! So handsome, with dark hair, blue eyes, well dressed. When we knelt for the prayer, his hand brushed mine. Just for a second. And it was like an electric current passed through my body. Lit me up just like a Christmas tree! My face got so hot. And my good blue dress was sticking to me! After the service he disappeared. I asked but no one knew him. He was a stranger, a tall, good-looking stranger. But you know what? I saw him again. At the Top Dollar Bar and Grill. He was so bold. He came right up to me and introduced himself, and said he was looking to meet a good woman. So, we started going out all the time after that. He was a little short of money, so most times I paid. I didn't mind. He was new in town, and hadn't made the right connections yet. Oh people talked, I know they did.

One day, Charles took me in his arms and asked me to marry him. I tell you, my heart started racing. Because I knew I'd found the man for me. So, I started making wedding plans. Charles had to take a short trip to clear up some old business. I gave him $3,000 for the trip. Then he phoned and said the car had broken down. So I wired him some more. Then he called from Florida and said he'd found a lovely piece of land that we could build our dream home on. It was going for a song. And I'd finally be able to get out of this stinking town. We needed to put down $20,000 to hold the deal. So I went to the bank. He promised to call me. I waited by that phone all night and the next day and the one after that. I thought maybe he'd had a terrible accident and was dying by the side of the road. No such luck. You know, I didn't mind losing the money as much as I hated being laughed at. And all the old biddies at the church looking at me like I had it coming. So I stopped going out. Had all my groceries delivered. Now I just sit in the dark. I can still hear all of his fancy words. It's like they're on a tape that keeps playing inside my head. Oh, hell! I know I should forget him. But I just can't shake this feeling. This gnawing, deep inside. It's like a mouse crawled into my mouth while I was sleeping, and now it's eating away inside me.

So, one night as I was lying there, I got this crazy notion. I got up and dug out all of his stuff, clothes and shoes. I dragged it all out to the brick barbecue out back. Soaked it in gasoline, tossed in a match and stepped back to watch the memory of that man go right up in smoke. I was just about to throw on the last pair of pants when something fell out. An address book. Full of women's names.

So I started calling them all up. You know he'd conned over a hundred women? He'd searched out the ones who were divorced or widowed and then he made his move. And I was just another easy mark. If you catch him, you let me know. I'm going to call up all those women again. We'll have us a little get together. A surprise party! Each one of us will get to be alone with him for five minutes. That's all it'll take.

***

Available as a copyscript.

Toast

Allan Stratton

Emily, about fifty, is trying to communicate with the ghost of her dead lover.

EMILY

Loudon? Are you there? Loudon? If you're there please give me a sign? I want to see you. I need to see you. Please? You're still angry with me, aren't you? Why did you have to die angry with me? Why? You didn't let me explain. You didn't give me a chance to say l was sorry. You just died. You just died and I came in to work the next day with a new silk tie, the kind you liked, all gift wrapped with a card to say I was sorry, I didn't mean it, only they said you weren't coming in and you'd never be coming in again and I wouldn't be able to see you anymore. And I wouldn't be able to say I was sorry. And I hate you for leaving me like that. Dear God, Loudon, my last memory of you is of you sitting there with that hurt look in your eyes and me slamming the door. It isn't fair, damnit. It isn't fair. I loved you. (*pause*) You used to tease me. You called me a Baptist prude. Well maybe I don't wear dresses that leave nothing to the imagination. But I don't know many Baptist prudes who check into the Park Plaza with a married man. For twenty years, I lived in terror I'd bump into somebody from church or the bridge club. I'd go up the elevators and walk through the halls pretending to read *The Globe and Mail*. You thought it was funny. But I didn't think it was funny. It went against everything I believed. But inside those rooms...those were the happiest days of my life. Of course, you were always in a hurry. The first time, I thought the cabby must be outside with the meter running. Heaven's to Betsy, I barely had time to turn out the lights before you let out a holler, rolled over and snored. I didn't think it had happened. Except it hurt. I was convinced sex was like amnesia with a dentist. It was two years before I figured out what all the fuss was about...I'll never forget the day I put my foot down. "I'm a Baptist, dammit. You make me feel like a two-bit whore. It's her or me." And when you said you weren't going to divorce her, it tore me apart. You always hurt the ones you love. Shakespeare has nothing on

The Mills Brothers. I'll never understand. After everything you said. After everything you promised. I stormed out of this office with you looking like a deer caught in the headlights.

I went to the funeral. And I sat in the back with the other employees. And no one suspected. Nobody knew. Jane said, "Oh yes, you're the secretary with the spelling problems, aren't you, dear? So glad you could come." I wanted to smack her. I wanted to shout, "Who do you think reminded the big lug about your anniversaries, you little toad? Who do you think bought your Christmas gifts?" I wanted to scream, "You don't know what it is to grieve. You put on a show with your big fake tears, but you're waving good-bye with a VISA card." I wanted to be cruel and ugly and horrible. I wanted her to feel the pain I felt. But mostly I wanted to hold you. I wanted to kiss you good-bye. But I couldn't.

We were never alone. All I could do was straighten your tie when no one was looking. You were so fussy about your ties. And it was so crooked. I bet Jane did it for spite. Dear God, you've given me so much. But the one thing I want is the one thing I can't have. I want him. I want him. (*beginning to cry*) I want to feel him holding me. I want him not to be hurt. I want him not to be angry. But I want him to know I'm a human being. I want him to know I feel and hurt and rage and hate and love. I miss him so desperately. Please God, please. Wherever you are, if you are — Please let him know that I love him. Please let him know. (*wiping her eyes*) Aren't you the proper fool. You've lived your life for daydreams. I'm an old boozer, that's what I am. As if anyone cares for a Baptist prude.

***

Available from the author - contact Playwrights Union of Canada.

Someday

Drew Hayden Taylor

Anne Wabung, a Native woman, had her daughter taken away by Children's Aid workers when the girl was only a toddler. It is Christmas 35 years later, and Anne's yearning to see her now-grown daughter is stronger than ever. When the family is finally reunited however, neither woman's dreams are fulfilled.

ANNE

..."suitable." My home wasn't suitable. What the heck do they know about what makes a home? I clothed you. I fed you. I loved you. Out here that was suitable. When that investigator woman stood there in my own kitchen not a foot from where you're sitting right now — when she stood there and said I'd been abandoned and I asked her what she was talking about anyways and she said right to my face that I was a woman whose husband walked right out on her — I wanted to yell in her face, "Yes I have a man and he didn't run out on me. He's a fine man gone to join the army to keep peace in this world and he sends me and his baby money." That's what I wanted to say to that...investigator woman from the Children's Aid. But I couldn't. Frank made me promise on the Bible not to, no matter what. He said it might get us in trouble. We got in trouble anyway. They took my little Grace right out of my arms and I never saw her again after that terrible day God help me. They wouldn't even tell me where they took you. And poor Frank when he got back and found out what happened went drinking for four days. He'd never done that before. I almost lost it then but one of us had to be strong so I was strong for the both of us.

***

Published by Fifth House Publishers.

Zinni's Colour

Paula Wing

Marion, mid-fifties, has just returned from a trip to the South Seas. She sits in a cemetery, surrounded by her bags, by the grave of her husband. she recounts a story she heard on her trip.

MARION

There they were, Al! Out on the ocean, the high seas, all alone. Just the two of them and they were young too. They'd saved up the money and bought the boat and they were just going to travel around the world together. Picture it. And you can't sleep on those ocean passages, or at least not for long, because someone always has to be awake — to navigate or something. Anyway, they'd been out about two weeks, water water everywhere...and late one afternoon she says, 'I think I'll go make dinner,' and he says, 'I think I'll do some fishing', and she goes below to cook and he gets his fishing gear and then time passes. I don't know how much time, Al, because on the high seas nobody bothers to wear a watch. That how you measure things out there. But in the unspecified time that passes, she gets dinner together. Some baked thing. And when it's ready she puts two servings on two plates and she pours two glasses of wine and she puts the whole thing on a tray and comes upstairs. And he's gone. Poof! Just like that.

She stands there with the tray, listening to the silence...and she knows that if you fall off the boat on the high seas, you're dead. She's alone, Al, in the middle of the Pacific Ocean, flat alone. Two weeks from land, three hundred and thirty-six hours from sleep and he's dead somewhere back there, lungs exploded but she can't think about that yet. So. She puts down the tray with all the dinner things and she turns the boat around. Even though there's no possible hope of finding him. Even though she doesn't even know how long he's been out there. She looks for him as hard as she can, so she won't have to think about the rest of this trip, or the rest of her life, which, all of a sudden, is happening *right now*.

It makes sense when you think about it, Al. See, when all there is is ocean everywhere you look, your eye can't possibly pick out a little human head in all waves and swells. It's just too small.

So he's done for and she's looking for him anyway — and somehow she's not crying, her eyes are clear, and what do you think, Al? She sees him! She sees his head! And she brings the boat to him and she pulls him safely on board. You can see them clinging to each other, can't you?

The thing is, he's still got his fishing rod and he's hooked this tuna. And when she finally says, 'What happened?' he says, 'Well...I was fishing and I got this big tuna on the end of the line and I went to reel it in and, I don't know, we hit a swell or something and — I didn't even have time to scream...I'm treading water like hell and I know I'm gonna die, this is really it, but suddenly, then I feel this tug on the line so I just concentrate, as hard as I can, on reeling in that fish. And just at the moment when I had him and there was nothing left to do but wait to drown...I saw you.'

And then you know what they did, Al? Then they threw the baked something overboard and they ate that tuna for dinner. I can't stop thinking about it. Imagine what that tuna tasted like.

***

Available from the playwright - contact Playwrights Union of Canada.

Intimate Admiration

Richard Epp

In a health resort in Badenweiler, Germany, Olga Knipper, star of the Moscow Art Theatre, has watched her husband, Anton Chekhov, die. With his body beside her in the room, she recalls the events of his passing.

OLGA

(*warmly, with a sense of humour*) I stayed with him until morning. The doctor came and went, and I notified the management. 'Dead? But this is a health spa. People don't die here.' They waited all day to remove the body. 'No one must see.' At midnight two pimple-faced German boys took him out in a laundry basket. He didn't quite fit.

We had a small service in Badenweiler. I insisted, despite what he would have said. And then we boarded a train for Russia. At the border they put him in an old green railway car marked 'Oysters'. Imagine.

In Moscow his procession wound its way to the Art Theatre where there were eulogies, performances really, applause. The crowds were so thick around the doors that his brother Michael and his sister Masha had to prove who they were to get in. Poor Masha. She is sometimes misunderstood.

I remember there was a military funeral the same day. Some people followed the wrong procession. More crowds at the cemetery: students, peasants who overran the markers to get near his grave and to throw their flowers. (*she allows herself a moment of tender remembrance*) So many flowers.

Years later we moved him again. From the family plot to the artists' corner. To be remembered with the actors of the Moscow Art Theatre. He would have laughed. He would. He loved a good joke.

(*turning to him*) So, now you are an author. You are an author and I am an actress. We were drawn together in a fascinating whirlpool. I lived joyously like a child. I loved you and dreamed of fame. And in the morning I woke up singing.

***

Available as a copyscript.

$\mathcal{D}$ancing $\mathcal{B}$ackwards

Aaron Bushkowsky

*Doris, a proud, independent former dance instructor in her fifties
practices dancing in her living room. She shows the early signs of
Alzheimer's Disease, but her memory of the past is still intact.*

DORIS

Being in love. What a wonderful feeling! Like every day is Christmas.
(*beat*) Albert didn't really like dancing all that much but he did try.
We went to this barn dance, actually called a barn waltz, five miles out
of town in a hay loft, of all things!

Everything was magical, the music, the hot wine, the company, the
smell of the hay. I wanted the night to go on forever. Albert didn't last
long, though, as much as he tried. Said he couldn't catch his breath for
the life of him. Eventually he disappeared outside for another cigarette.
When I found him he was standing outside this aluminum tool shed
under this pale blue light bulb. Albert had his coat collar turned up. At
first he didn't see me. I stood away from him in the middle of this
immense farm yard. I could hear the music from the barn behind me,
the snow ticking as it swirled against the shed, Albert wheezing
between all this.

When he finally did see me, he quickly threw away the cigarette, smiled
a little and opened his arms. You know what he said? He said, "Come
on, dearie, I can't see you. Come into the light. Come into the light."
And so I did. Even then, though, I felt him trembling. His heart
pounding away like a scared rabbit. He held my hand. Touched my face.
I could see his veins. They stood out...like...like blue rivers on the
moon.

It wasn't long after that, someone told a joke on Thanksgiving, of all
things, and Al couldn't stop coughing. His eyes watered over and...and,
well, that was that. We packed up and went straight to the hospital,

exactly one day before our seventh anniversary. (*beat*) Lucky, lucky number seven.

***

Available as a copyscript.

Coming of Age

Patricia Ludwick

Walking through life in seven-year stages, the Middle-aged Woman is stuck at seven-times-seven, balancing precariously on one leg between an Old Woman and a Young Woman. With their help she eventually learns to see through surfaces to the living flame of spirit — to shake up the old bag of bones and dance.

MIDDLE-AGED WOMAN

I can't for the life of me remember what I came in here for. What was I doing? I came into the middle of my life and I...I was just going to — I was going to get some financial counselling, plan my retirement, invest in real estate. I was just going to learn to paint, to play the flute, I was going to go to Nepal, I was going to — I was just going to — switch careers, move to the country, do what I want for a change but what the hell was — Retrace my steps, let my body remind me, remind, my body is somewhere between...zero and infinity. Maybe I should just stay here. I could just stay right here and...I could dye my hair, I could have a face lift, treat myself to a week at a spa? I could do some of those slamdunk thigh exercises, uhhhh, maybe just carry more weight when I do my fast walking so I can stay here on one leg somewhere between...

I could get a new wardrobe, long flowing elegant clothing that barely suggests the body underneath. Keep my chin up so the jowls don't show. Wear long, dangling earrings to distract the eye. Try a very subtle but complex perfume. So I can just stay here, balancing somewhere between...This is exhausting. Calm down. Do some yoga, install a Jacuzzi, learn some new stress management techniques. As long as I breathe deeply, I can stay here for years, balancing not exactly young but not — but what was I doing? I'm right here, in the middle of my life, the same person I've always been — I'll just carry on doing what I've always done, wash the dishes, sweep the floor, do the laundry because if I don't, if I stop doing...I have to go shopping. I have as usual forgotten my list. I walk into the grocery store and I'm going to buy — what? Food? Cleaning supplies? Company? I am an ordinary woman. Walking. Where thousands have walked before me. Leaving no footprints. Keep walking, just keep walking because walking is good for you, keep walking to keep fit. Fit for what? I can't even find my glasses.

***

Available from the author - contact Playwrights Union of Canada.

A Play About the Mothers of Plaza de Mayo

Alisa Palmer

A mother writes a series of letters to her "disappeared" daughter in Argentina.

DOLORES

The Mothers are celebrating their fifteenth anniversary. We will have a conference at the Ricoleta Cultural Centre. Who would have thought. The richest part of town. My life has taken a direction that I never could have imagined. I give lectures, I give interviews. I talk a lot. People want to hear the story, from all different countries. I tell them. There are streets named after us in three cities in Spain. There are parks named after us in Holland. And schools called the Mothers of Plaza de Mayo. They are even building one in Argentina in Lujan. We have received prizes for The Struggle, for Liberty, for Justice. People visit our office from all over the world, artists, lawyers, journalists. People write doctorates. Parliamentarians, church representatives, and women's groups. Human rights groups invite us to Europe. We have support groups in Spain, Italy, Germany, and Canada, who invite us to meet with them. We have edited three books of our own poetry. People have done operas and plays. Only one film, that I know of. Liv Ullman was in it. It was quite good. There was *The Official Story*, but that was about the Grandmothers. It was much too sentimental. What has happened should be public property. That is supposed to be the point.

I don't know what good it is doing. The Generals are free, and laws have been invented to ensure that they can never be tried again. I come home alone Thursdays after the Plaza. My feet swelling up. Fewer and fewer people go. Some of us can't go on much longer. Soon it will be a cavalcade of wheelchairs and crutches. Some people say we should stop. Some of the Mothers have already left. They feel enough has been done. I'm not sure. I'm not ready to take off my kerchief yet. I wore it when the generals were tried, and I didn't take it off when they were charged. I wanted to wait and see what would happen next. Good thing too, because I wouldn't have had time to take it off and put it back on again before they were pardoned. I was still wearing my kerchief when that box of bones arrived with your name printed on the label. And I wore it when I took the box back, and put it in the hands of that stranger who didn't seem to understand why I wouldn't bury them. I'm not ready to stop, but I forget sometimes why I should continue. I wonder what there is left to say that I haven't said already. Even most of this letter has already been published in one of our books. In a week it will be the fifteenth anniversary of your disappearance. Around this time the other Mothers are always particularly patient with me. Especially Mrs. Ragne, who is such a lonely soul, in spite of all those grandchildren. I think in the end her daughter only made it as far as Peru. None of us know how they managed to track her down. You probably know. Mrs. Deluz was certainly quiet on the issue. That's no proof of anything, but the day I see her drag herself to the Plaza is the day I apologize for every bad thing I've thought about her. Teresa. I don't know if you would recognize me any more except that I am more like you.

***

Available as a copyscript.

Creation - The Mystery Cycle

Peter Anderson

Sarah, in front of the desert tent she shares with Abraham, laments her childlessness.

SARAH

Every woman in the world
Is pregnant, every tree bears fruit;
But one, whose leaf is dried and curled.
Inside of me Death spreads its roots.
Where and how has life gone wrong;
      It's like a joke,
      My life's a joke,
An empty, hopeless, bitter song.

How many years now has it been?
Each month I wait as days go by
And hope begins to rise again,
But each month's hope turns out a lie
And all my dreams end in despair.
      How many years,
      How many tears,
Of waking to the same nightmare?

I'm so worn out, the hole's so deep;
I wish that everything was done,
I wish that I could fall asleep
And not wake up, not face the sun.
I feel so old and hopeless, hardened.
      My life's been haunted;
      All I wanted
Was a child, a home, a garden,

A place where I could help things grow;
Not this dry and barren place,
This desert plain where all one sows
Comes up a stunted, blighted waste.

***

Available as a self-cover paperback.

Magpie

Kit Brennan

Bernice is large, middle-aged, and prone to fantasies. Her small-town life is disrupted by the arrival of a gifted dance instructor. He is everything she aspires to be, and everything that her upbringing has rejected as frivolous. As a result, her fantasy world spirals into a desperate, croaking lie.

BERNICE

Oh...I always wanted to fly. Always. I was made for flight.

It's this eating disorder, that's what the problem is. I can't eat, I get so thin I can't get off the ground, I'm too weak. I eat like a bird, can't keep nothing down. He told me, he said you've got to eat, Bernice, you're too thin, you're going to blow away in the next big wind. And I laughed and said don't worry about me. I'll be fine, and he said to me he said, me not worry? You're all I think about, you're what I live for, you are, you're my princess in her ivory tower, on her glass mountain, in her copper castle. You're my china figurine. That's the kind of things he says, my teacher. He's my dancing teacher. He loves me true. He does. No matter what they say, I believe in him, he'd never forsake me. Never.

Come back! Come back come back come back!

Come back...

> *She pulls out a bag of potato chips, eats mechanically.*

That man that came earlier? That Dave? He's just a man I buy food for, I don't know him. He lives in a trailer park. There's this little kitchen and a tiny refrigerator, and he expects me to put food on the table for him and five kids. Five! Where they all came from I couldn't tell you.

Oh yes, they're mine. They're mine all right; I just don't remember what led up to their arrival. You must think I'm lying to you, but honest to God it's that forgettable. I remember the feeling inside, I remember them growing and the way my body felt, I remember their births, the first's head all lumpy from the forceps, my last one slipping out like a seal — those things I remember like it was yesterday, each one of them separate, but him. Him I don't recall.

I'm not ready for that. I've told them. I can't keep nothing down.

I walk up and down the aisles. I put food in the basket, I figure out what to make. I pay with his money. I'm forced to serve them, you know, it's like my penance, but all the time I know some day soon some beautiful morning they're going to wake up and I won't be there any more. He will have taken me away. He's coming and they'd better get used to it because the face of the world is going to be changed. And it's a strain, knowing and never telling, never letting on the things you know inside are about to happen, never letting even the tiniest little explosion of joy and expectation escape your lips because they're jealous and they'll try to stop you, they can't stand to see true love, true sexuality. They can't stand it.

> *She crumples the empty bag.*

Born and bred Presbyterian, eh? But there you go. I got an open mind. I like to know what's going on, what other people think. My Ma'd die if she knew. You're the only girl, Bernice, we got to keep them going right, we got to keep the faith. What'll people think, you not there every Sunday? They're not going! How come I got to go! I been away from home over half my life — funny how the years go. How she keeps her hold. Never kept it over my brothers, drinkin' and swearin'. Just goes to show.

***

Available as a copyscript.

Dispossessed

Aviva Ravel

Roochel recalls her lover, a man she worked for as an operator in his factory. That was many years ago, in the 1930s, when she was a new immigrant.

ROOCHEL

I was so young, I had nobody.
He asked me to go to the movies,
He bought me a milk-shake, chocolate,
When he brought me home he kissed me.
I asked him to come in,
He didn't want,
I begged him.
It's frightening to be alone.
There were rats in the walls,
Everything creaked,
The floor, the ceiling, the cupboards,
I can't sleep alone.
In the old country I slept with my sister,
So I begged him,
he came in.
He stayed the whole night,
He said he would marry me.
He came home with me a whole month.
It was the best month of my life.
One month like that is worth a lifetime.
He made love like a poet.
When he breathed on me,
the breath was so strong,
it could push a thousand boats from
one end of the ocean to the other.
When his fingers touched my skin,
the sun inside my belly burned,
And I melted like butter over the fire,

When he was inside my body,
the whole city burst into fire,
and it rolled all over the mountain,
even the river could not put it out.
It was fire and water, water and fire,
and no air, never any air,
We choked together, we died together,
but each morning we woke up,
It was a miracle.

Then one day he said it's no use,
The father's cousin has a daughter,
The daughter will inherit money from the mother when she marries.
The business needs money or it will go bankrupt,
So he has to marry the cousin's daughter
so they won't go bankrupt.
It was no use crying,
He didn't like tears,

He said that one month
should last a lifetime,
He was right, it did.

I know why he didn't marry me,
He was ashamed to bring me to his family.
With my accent I didn't look too good,
I had no education, no clothes, nothing.
He had a classy family,
A real Canadian family from 1866,
He had a car, a degree, and a big house,
I had nothing.

I never saw him again.
I changed my job,
And the next thing I know I have a belly,
I was happy, yes.
All the time the baby was inside my belly,
I was happy.
I thought maybe if he saw the baby
He would change his mind.
I should have known
that money has a mind of its own.

I can still feel your body,
the hard shoulders,
the hair on your arms,
the strong hands,
especially your smell,
like burnt toast.
I feel you all over me
and all around me.
I am floating into you
like that lonely cloud
and disappearing into the sky.

I wanted to put the baby in the snow
And leave it there,
But I saw God's hand in the sky
so I figure there's a purpose to all this,
Now I know there was no purpose,
It was a trick to punish me,
So I kept the baby,
And got poor Seymour to help me,
so there should be a man in the house sometimes.
I never wanted to marry,
I hated all men,
I never trusted no man again,
I gave it all to him,
I had no love left for no one,
But I trusted Seymour,
because he loved me
and I didn't love him.
That's what I had over him,
A whole lifetime he tries to make me love him,
As long as a man tries, a woman is safe,
A woman should never show too much love to a man

She should keep it to herself,
So she'll never get hurt.
I was hurt, so I learned.

***

Published by Playwrights Canada Press in "Women Write for Theatre,
Volume 2".

If We Are Women

Joanna McClelland Glass

*Two grandmothers, a daughter, Jessica, and a granddaughter
gather on the deck of a beach house. The three older women
discuss their pasts, their present and are confounded by the
granddaughter's decision to disregard all that she's heard. Jessica
has just lost her lover of many years, and here, Rachel, her
mother-in-law, from her previous marriage, wonders why she
came to her aid.*

RACHEL

How odd, to be here now. To drive up, four hours from Pennsylvania,
to be at her side in her hour of grief. But I came willingly, as I always
have. I came after the divorce when she was alone with the children and
struggling for money. I mended and patched, I made slip-covers to hide
the damage of kids and cats. And after Fleming arrived, I still came. I
cooked for the four of them, my daughter-in-law, my two grandchildren,
and the landscape painter. I cooked the old, Jewish dishes they requested.
Blintzes and borsht, latkes, kreplach, challa, hamantashen. My friends
think I've kept this relationship alive for my grandchildren. They think,
because I could see my son in the kids' faces, I wouldn't mind serving
up latkes to the invading landscape painter. They're wrong.

There's something in her life that's forever...(*shrugging*)...magnetic.
And, repellent. Magnetic because her writing is so mysterious. I've
thought if I could locate the source, the wellspring that propels her pen,
I, too, might write. Why can't I? I love language, I express myself
well. Perhaps I know too much. I'd read all of Shakespeare by the time
I was twenty. I've taught the classics, I've read reams of criticism. But
when I sit down to blank paper, my pen is paralyzed. (*an introspective
pause*) Her source is her feelings. Deeply, zealously felt feelings. Her
profession is, essentially, one of confession. That's what's repellent. It's
not my pen that's paralyzed, it's me. I'm ill-at-ease with the zealously
felt. Gerald was, too...not surprising. The hand that rocks the cradle. He
learned at my knee that people impaled on their feelings never achieve

maturity. And I was right. There is something severely...arrested about Jess.

How odd to be here now, while she mourns the man who wasn't my son.

***

Published by Playwrights Canada Press.

Goodbye Marianne

Irene K. Watts

11-year-old Marianne has been sent to safety from Nazi Germany. Her parents do not survive. As she unpacks in her new home, she finds a last letter from her mother.

MRS. KOHN

My Dearest Daughter, I close my eyes and imagine you in your new home. You're unpacking, you place the photograph of the three of us on your dresser, you put your favourite book, it's still "Emil and the Detective" isn't it?, by your bed. You open the envelope to read my letter, I'm going to put it under the picture frame, so you'll find it right away; perhaps you sit on the window seat to read it, I'm sure your new bedroom has a window. Does it look over fields, or mountains, is snow falling?

Clothes are scattered everywhere on the floor around me, no, don't cry my darling, you would laugh and tease to see your Mother in such a muddle. I want to put everything you love and need into this one small suitcase. Another cruelty, they allow you to take only what you can carry. How proud you were when Daddy bought this case for your tenth birthday. We didn't guess then that only one year later I would have to try and cram a lifetime of possessions into it. I hope someone helped you carry the case from the train to the ship, but knowing my independent daughter, I'm sure you would not allow anyone to touch it. I'm writing this in your old room, Marianne, you are all around me. I never want to finish packing, it is the hardest and the best thing I have ever had to do. How can I tell you how I feel? I folded your heavy ski sweater, in the bottom of the case, then I took it out to make room for your long winter scarf and gloves. Canada is so cold they say, I put the sweater back and took out last year's blue party dress, you said it's too childish. You are growing so fast, and I won't be there to let down the hem of your clothes. Do you wonder, "How can they send me away? What kind of parents do that?" I must find the right words to help you understand. Remember how I nagged you to keep silent in the street, to look away from the uniforms, to keep your head down, not to make jokes, not to make friends?

This is not a way to grow up. The days will seem silent without your chatter. I know I will long for one of our silly battles, long to hear you answer me back, long to complain about my messy daughter, long to hug you. Marianne, I send you away for a chance for life, just a life. There isn't one here for us, I cannot keep you safe. I send you away because I love you, I send you with love and hope for a future. Goodbye, Marianne.

***

Published by Scirocco Drama.

$\mathcal{H}$omeward $\mathcal{B}$ound

Elliott Hayes

In this dark comedy, Bonnie and Glen have called their entire, squabbling family together to tell them that Glen is terminally ill and has decided to take his own life to end his suffering and that of his family.

BONNIE

I'm not sure at what point my emotional detachment began. I mean, I'm sure that I do look cold...about...things. But...l don't really know what I think I feel anymore — because I know I "think" I feel and maybe I don't. Feel.

It all gets so clouded over the years...words started losing their sting at some point in time, you know...in your lifetime...in my lifetime too, for that matter....God knows when...you could pick any date in this century and it wouldn't matter...but you see, our ability to feel anything is bound to our ability to express it and my talking about it sounds muddy because my thoughts are muddy and my thoughts are muddy because I can't say what I mean. Because we don't think the way we used to anymore. I mean caring about what words really mean. What they do...well, we just don't think like that, anymore.

We're cold. Cold-er.

Not that it matters now. Because it doesn't. It — this — just happened. Like everything just happens.

So what if Nick almost burned down the garage and I thought it was Chris Thing-me all these years? I already hated that kid because of what he tried to do to Norris in the Thomas' storm cellar. Fellatio.

Remember that word? What is it now? Why am I pretending I don't know? Blow job.
That's the word, isn't it? The term. When a woman takes a man's penis in her mouth. Or a man does. Like my son. Who does that. I mean I

know he does, whether or not I like to think he does. Knowing and thinking are very different things, aren't they? And if we think about it, we know a hell of a lot more than we want to. Don't we? Who cares, of course.

Everybody's got a bubble in them, Dr. Meissner says. Said. And it can only take up so much room before it forces whatever we are out. So now when he's asleep and I'm not, I lie there and think that Glen's got a bubble in him. A bubble like in Double Bubble bubble gum, just waiting for God to blow into it. Is God like that?

Is God that banal?

When I think about it in those terms I have to put the other God out of my mind. You know, the God like the painting in the Sistine Chapel.

Big God, little man. Painted by a man who took a man's penis in his mouth at the behest of a pope. (*beat*)

The painting was a behest I mean.

But it does make you think, doesn't it?

***

Published by Playwrights Canada Press.

Betty Mitchell

Kenneth Dyba

Betty Mitchell, the famed Canadian acting teacher, sits in her favourite over-stuffed armchair, sipping her never-absent rye and water, chain-smoking. At eighty years old, her voice is deeply weathered, her diction precise, her delivery theatrical. She gestures grandly to an imposing statue in the corner.

BETTY

Yes, the Nike of Samothrace...The Winged Victory of Samothrace...a beautiful thing, isn't it?

She drinks, smokes and smiles.

Well, you see, darling, I did a play at Western High. Wilder's *Our Town*; in 1942, with Conrad Bain and Nana Canning and all my other children. It was such a beautiful play.

You know, parents sometimes criticized my choice of plays being too "sophisticated" for their little children. Well, we considered having the heroine die of cancer instead of childbirth but since most of us had arrived here by childbirth, we finally decided not to tamper with Mr. Wilder.

Conrad was sixteen or so at the time and I will never forget him. Of course I'm a great Stanislavskyite — I like this interior acting which I "larned" my young people.

You know how that stage in western is. Well, Conrad used to come up from the basement where he had put his make-up on, up all those stairs, and I was on the rise at the back — to see that everything was in order: Mother Hen Me. All of sixteen years of age was Conrad. he would go across the stage, up the stairs at the back, to the top of the lighting booth where he had a mat...and what he did up there to transform himself I'll never know. He was playing Wilder's Stage Manager.

Finally he would come down from there when the call went.

"Places! Places, please!

And he would come down from there all of seventy years of age and he would walk right by me and his eyes were *old* eyes. He used to go down and stand by the right proscenium. He has the most beautiful voice. I'll never forget it.

> Well, the name of our town is Grover's Corner, New Hampshire — just across the Massachusetts line. The time is just before dawn. The sky is beginning to show some streaks of light over in the East, there, behind the mountains. The morning star gets wonderful bright the minute it has to go.

And then in the third act...

> You come up here on a fine afternoon and you can see range on range of hills — awful blue they are...

I used to weep every time he said it. "Awful blue they are."

There was a teacher named Catherine Barclay. She taught French at Western. She loved that play so much she came to every performance. She came back from Paris the summer after we did the play and she carried this Winged Victory by hand — it's enormously heavy — and she gave it me for the pleasure our play had given her. And she would always tell me how she could smell the beautiful colours. Well, of course, there were no roses in the play, no rain. We pantomimed everything. But we, all of us, believed in the roses, in the rain. And so thus did our audience. That was my victory — those roses. And this is the Victory Catherine gave me.

> *She sits smoking, eyes bright.*

***

Available from the author - contact Playwrights Union of Canada.

Two Times Twenty

Ann Lambert

The speaker is a 70-year-old francophone, Corrine, talking to her daughter, Louise.

CORRINE

Old? You think you're getting old ? You don't know what old is. (*beat*) Why do you writers always want to know how it was...how we were? We all had 20 inch waists and boobs big enough to fill a bra...and beautiful brown hair. All my sisters and I. We were all beautiful. Well, maybe not Matante Lucille. She was, okay, she was a bit homely. But the rest of us...we knew how to live then. We weren't so dull that we had to watch other people on T.V. all day long. (*beat*) We used to sing...Giselle had a beautiful voice, like honey...Papa would play the piano and our boyfriends would come to call. If they were too eager, Papa hated that...your father never was...but he was English and Protestant so he didn't stand a chance anyway. There's power, you know, when the situation is hopeless. Don't get me going on that. (*beat*) We never thought we'd be old. (*beat*) But that's not what I wanted to tell you. I want to tell you you should write about now. About what is.

We had our knitting club luncheon last week. It's just once a year...this time it was Matante Collette's turn. What a feast she put out...you know Collette. We ate too much, we're all fat anyway. I get fatter and fatter. I don't care. Except your Matante Lucille. She stopped eating and got so skinny her neck sticks out like a chicken's. There's nothing left of her! Why should I stop eating what I want? (*beat*)...No, we don't knit. We've never actually knitted. We call our gang *"les vielles pelottes."* Well, it means a ball of wool. What's happened to your French?...But it also means...never mind. It's a bit rude. Look it up in your dictionary. Collette served *paté de fois gras* she makes herself...you know Collette...St. André cheese...ragout with real pig's knuckles. We ate like...pigs. Except Lucille...she never eats. No. She cries. Because Pierre, her husband, has started going to mass again every morning...and he won't have sex with her...we still like to have sex! Your father couldn't for so many years but that doesn't — *Ben, voyons donc!* You're grown up now...we can talk about this...(*beat*) The husbands die...or got to mass...or watch...golf all day long. They're weak...I don't know why. Maybe they worked too hard at something they didn't like. Maybe because they didn't have the children...kids make you tough. You'll see when you have your own...of course you're gonna have children. Don't be ridiculous! (*beat*) At least, we still try. That's why I can't listen to Lucille anymore. *En tous cas...*

Collette is serving lunch...and everything is just perfect..you know Collette. Lucille is criticizing our children...Oh, she always does that. Hers are such a mess that it makes her feel better. Pierre is at the detox farm again, and Lisanne is pregnant again. No one, least of all Lisanne, knows who the father is. Lucille will end up raising another baby, and she needs that like she needs to have another heart attack...No, I am not going to quit smoking. It's too late for that now. Because I like it! I know life isn't over! But people keep treating us like it is. You turn 65 and suddenly no one's listening anymore. Nobody takes us seriously... it's like being children again. Waiters call me dear now...all the time...I've never been a dear and I'm not going to start now.

After the lunch, Collette went to get the cognac...and...Lucille is still crying, she's a bit drunk now. The doctor has her on Prozac, so doped up she leaves her house in her nightie half the time. Anyway...Giselle gets up from the sofa to get more food, and it's not easy, and, she weighs 200 pounds now, and with her leg...and there's this...odor. We look down at the sofa, and there's a huge stain. Oh, the smell! Giselle is in the kitchen...we don't know what to do...Giselle who wore white gloves every day...Giselle who never leaves the house uncoiffed... Giselle who scrubbed her floors and her kids within an inch of their lives...who never liked sex because she couldn't stand her own smell...Giselle whose life is perfect...everyone else has problems... *Imagine toi!* Pissed herself. Everywhere. So, we didn't say anything. Collette got a towel, and covered it up...Giselle comes back, like nothing happened. Pours the tea from the silver pot my mother left her...Collette starts to giggle. And giggle. Lucille doesn't know what's going on, but she joins in too. And me, I laughed and laughed so much I thought I'd get angina again. Giselle acted as though nothing had happened. (*pause*) That's it. I don't know why I told you that. There's nothing there. (*beat*). It wasn't cruel! It's not so sad...that's old age. Pissing your pants, and you don't even know it...(*beat*) I wake up everyday and look at that face that isn't mine anymore, and hope...it never happens to me. (*beat*) Inside, I still see a 19-year-old girl...singing with my beautiful sisters around the family piano...just beginning my life.

***

Available from the author - contact Playwrights Union of Canada.

Men

The Gospels Accordingly

Fabrizio Filippo

The play centres on an Italian-Canadian family of cousins at the annual family New Year's Eve party in Woodbridge, Ontario (outside Toronto), in the basement recreation room. One of the cousins, Joseph, has been charged with the rape and murder of a prostitute in Toronto, and has been on the run for about four months. He returns to explain his actions. Here, his cousin Enzo, recalls an incident from their youth.

ENZO

When we were twelve, Joseph had this idea to build a clubhouse on the roof of the school because nobody went there. So we built these pulleys. Joseph got an idea for pulleys from how they built cathedrals; which was one of the things we were studying in class. We scrounged up all the lumber we could find and attached it to the pulleys and yanked them up. The janitor shows up, we panic, drop all the wood and Joseph takes a running jump off the school onto the field. He didn't hesitate or anything. Like he didn't care if he lived or died. I stop at the edge. He's screaming at me we don't have much time. Jump! Jump! I do. I jumped. Actually I sort of hang dropped. But I did it which was very important to me. So I'm falling and I'm thinking 'great!' 'This is amazing!' Then bang, I fell the wrong way. I couldn't run. Joseph tried to carry me, but we were twelve and I was heavier than he was. Then the janitor...what was his name? It was Faubern. (*not sure*) Mr. Fau-whatever catches us and all I think is how it's my fault we got caught. The janitor threatens to call the cops. Somehow Joseph convinces the guy to call Mrs. Everson, our teacher, instead. So Mrs. Everson comes down there and it's late Friday and she's pissed, she's steaming, until (*pausing for effect*)...she sees the pulleys. She — thinks — they're — marvelous. There were the greatest thing she ever saw. And she suddenly loves us. Why? Because those pulleys showed that we were listening in her class. She drove us each a block away from our houses and never said a word about it to us or anyone else...it's amazing.

***

Available from the author - contact the Playwrights Union of Canada.

Numbrains

Margaret Hollingsworth

*On the eve of his 17th birthday, a boy spends four days on a
West Coast beach guarding a beached Bowhead whale.*

BOY

It's so dark now, I'm dazzled and all I can make out is the wet sand,
covered with a film of water, sort of shimmering and this, like, hump,
this, like, huge fucking hulk out there and the little white crests of
waves licking. Like, licking. And she doesn't move. I sit.

After that I go back up the cliff by touch, it's a good thing I know the
way, and my bike's still there. And I ride like a pro, ninety miles an
hour, so I can get a sweater and a sleeping bag. I grab a two-litre Coke,
a pack of crackers and a bunch of cheese and I look for something that's
gonna give me some light.

> *He takes a flashlight, a couple of candles, and a
> welding torch out of his backpack.*

I dunno how to use this, (*the torch*) but if *he* (*meaning his father*) can
do it, it's got to be easy.

I jump back on the bike. When I get back to the cliff top I see the
beach is black. I shout hello and nobody answers.

I go down the long way this time, because I don't wanna leave my bike.
I carry it down the steps, and across the sand. There's no moon and I
keep sinking my feet in pools of water. She's still out there. I can feel
her. She's, like...breathing...I can hear these great, like...breaths...
pants...I dunno what you'd call them...the tide's way out now. She's on
her own. The water must be way past her. The sand's roughed up and
smoothed into waves. And I reach her, and she's lying there on her side.
Breathing. I got my bike and I'm gonna prop it up against her side. I
know you're not supposed to touch, but I figure she might not mind.

Not now. I don't do it. I don't know what to do. (*rummaging in his pack, he brings out a package of birthday cake candles and a box of matches and he lights a tiny candle tentatively*) Found these in the fridge. (*he tips the rest of the candles*) And there's a Sara Lee chocolate cake in the back of the freezer. Who does he think he's gonna surprise?

(*he sits and stares at the whale*) I wish I'd'a brought something to hold water. I could keep her wet. Well, not wet — damp. I could damp her down. Make her feel nice. I should get a hose or something. I should do something. I gotta keep her alive. I gotta keep her here until tomorrow when they come back. I don't know how to get that across.

Maybe I'd be best to just sit quiet and do nothing. Just let her know I'm here. Just let her hear me so she knows. (*long pause*) Don't feel right.

> *He lights a large candle and walks slowly towards the whale, candle in hand, singing.*

"As I was a walkin' the streets of Laredo
As I was a walkin' the streets one day,
I saw a young cowboy, all dressed in white linen..."

Nah. (*standing, he holds the candle aloft*) Her mouth's closed. Her eye's open (*squinting*) but you can't read it. You can't read nothing. It's just an eye. Just an itty bitty eye.

> *He stands very still, candle aloft, eyes closed.*

I feel it. All of a sudden I'm being lifted up. I'm on a level with the eye and the mouth's open, and I walk inside. I walk inside. Man. What a beauty. Long bones...from here to over there...(*waving into distance*). Long whale bones with this fine hair...like hay drying on poles...and my feet are like...sinking, sinking up to the ankles in krill. Spongy. Red. Brown. Millions of krill. All this dead ocean life. Undigested. And my feet are sinking in dead...or maybe it's alive. Like me. Or am I? And the baleen's moving. Sweeping and filtering. Sweeping and filtering...a fucking forest...and I know I'm gonna get filtered...it sweeps and I duck, sweep and duck. Hairy teeth. Bone plates and plates and plates and plates. Brown and red and grey and...I don't wanna hold up the light...I don't wanna set her on fire, even though she's wet, it's wet inside...it's a cave, a wet cave...it's a fuckin car wash, a car wash. It's like being at the bottom of the sea...but there might be gases. I don't wanna risk setting off the gases and maybe — Kaboom. (*he hugs the candle and blows it out*)

Hairy teeth. She's a baleen. A Bowhead. I'm standing here, inside...I dunno how it happened....*Balaema mysticus*. You don't get Bowheads outside the Arctic, right? They don't come this far south. And I'm up to my knees in plankton, copsods, mysids, amphipods, isopods, ptergrads, copsods, mysids, amphipods, isopods, ptergrads, copsods, mysids...up in the Arctic...they're up there in the Arctic. Maybe she thinks I'm a hunter. So she made a mistake...of course...bad radar...got confused. It doesn't happen. They gotta stop!

(*as dawn comes up*) They came back at crack of dawn next day. The engines woke me up. The boats.

I never heard her die. I musta fell asleep. They came back at the crack of dawn only it was too late. I knew it, the minute I opened my eyes.

* * *

Published by the Hawthorne Society, Victoria, B.C.

Jason

Betty Jane Wylie

*JASON is a "high-functioning" retarded young man who faces
a group interview with a jury of occupants in a subsidized
housing complex. He answers questions and tries to present
himself well but his honesty and trust cause him to tell more
than he has to.*

JASON

Why do I want to live here? That's a good question.
Because it's nice.
Because it's clean, yeah, clean.
Because there's no cockroaches, right? No roaches.
Because it's safe.
She says the other, the other place, the place we're in now isn't safe,
and she doesn't even know what happ— what happened. I didn't tell her.
I didn't tell no one. Anyone. She tells us go in the side door, so no one
both— bothers us — she? Ruth, Ruth, my counsellor, I told you, Ruth
is my counsellor. She says don't talk to no one there, they're rough and
they'll maybe hurt us so we don't, we don't talk. I never talked but it
happened anyway. I didn't tell her, though. She doesn't know. She
doesn't know how bad, how bad it is.

How bad is it? You don't want to hear this. You won't — you won't
like it. I don't think I should tell you. I didn't tell her.
Okay, I'll tell you, but you have to, have to promise not to, not to
tell. He said he'd kill me if I told.

No, not Bud. He, I don't know his name, the guy in the laun— laundry
room. I was stan— standing by the washers, just watch watching the,
uh, clothes go round and he came in, he says hi I say hi he says you
new here I say yeah. What you got he says. Nothin', I say, I don't got
nothin'. That's not good enough he says 'cuz I want somethin'. And I
laughed a little and looked at the clothes going round and then he had a
knife, a bright knife all sharp and pointed and he's holdin' a knife at me
and grabs my shirt and pushes me down down down till my knees hit, I

was on my knees on the floor. You got a mouth he says and he push—pushes the knife in my neck. Open it, he says. Open what? The door's open. I looked. Yeah, the door's open but nobody's coming. Open what I say, my fly he says. What? My zipper, stupid, open it, come on. So I reach, reached up and undid his zipper and he stuck out at me, he flapped out sticking at me and he says suck it and he pushes the knife harder at my neck and pushes in my face. Open it and suck he says. So I so I so I, I almost, I— it stuck in my mouth — it was hard to swallow I started to throw up not throw up but it felt like almost throwing up and then someone was coming footsteps coming in the hall. He scratches my neck with the knife and pushes me over and he says don't tell or I'll kill you and he's gone. I said I fell down.

Sex? You want me to talk about sex? What do you want to know? I like it a lot. In a way, I mean, some people don't like it and some people do and and if you had it when you were growing up with it and some people don't get it and some people miss it and sometimes they don't really want it. It means having kids and responsibility and having a whole family together. The feeling is great too. It turns you on a lot. You you should be crazy about the person you like, the person you fall in love with you. You should stay with and take care of them and sometimes I feel that way, I feel— well, not rejected, but sometimes I feel — whenever Sandi goes out of town, to vis— to visit her family, I always go over and see...someone else. Prob'ly that's upsetting to her. And if I did go— they say if you see a person and if you see the other person and if you go behind the other person's back that's two-timing and that isn't — that's pretty bad if you had a relationship with the same person for a long time, like whatever, how many years it is, so basically, it sounds like I should stay with Sandi. (*he nods, satisfied*) Good.

***

Available as a copyscript.

Maggie's Last Dance

Marty Chan

Jim, a high school sophomore during the 1970's, is at the first dance of the year, ready to rock and roll, but too nervous to do anything.

JIM

Francis Langley High School. First dance of the year. And Jim Bauer's got Saturday Night Fever. I'm hot. Even the Grade Eleven babes are checking me out. Well, they've got a lot to look at. Shirt — 100 per cent velour, V-necked. Opened just enough to reveal my two neatly groomed chest hairs. Pants — bell bottoms. Shoes — standard two-inch platforms. Clothes by Woolco. Attitude by Foreigner — "Cold as Ice." Keep playing it cool. Only nerds dance this early.

Later in the dance, Derrick Sackett and Helen Barbour slow dance to The Commodores "Three Times a Lady." Derrick's hand slides down to Helen's butt. She slides it up again. His other hand drops. Helen shoves it back. He tries again and again. It's like watching a perpetual drinking bird.

They distract me so much that I almost miss her arrival. The hottest girl in grade 10. Ella Givens. She's everything Joannie Cunningham is and more. If only I could be her Chachi. I've had this thing for her since we were seven. She scans the gym. I see her head flick in my general direction. Cool, she wants me. Got to make my move soon. Next song, I promise. Leo Sayer's "You Make Me Feel Like Dancing." A cool song. A danceable song. A song where couples are made. The other guys sense this. They launch from the safety of the bleachers. They want to glide like Tony Manero, but they shuffle like Tim Conway.

Still, they move closer to the promised land. If I wait, someone might ask her. I have to make my move now. I join the race everyone wants to win but no one wants to lead. I make it past the chaperone. Past groping couples. Past the volleyball line. Mid point. No turning back. I smell the sweet aroma of Pert wafting from her hair.

Breath gets short. Legs shaky. My zits on high-beam. Velour shirt suddenly feels very heavy. She looks at me. I make a right-angle turn and head to the punchbowl. I slug back two glasses of orange punch. Liquid courage. Okay, I'm going to do it now. I spin around to see...Christine McCoy. She flashes me a smile. The disco light bounces off her braces and blinds me. I look to the dancing couples.

Oh man, she's dancing with Stephen Nesbitt. Mr. Hockey, Basketball, Volleyball, Highest Marks in Grade Ten, Drives His Own Car. What's he got that I don't? He tells her a joke. She laughs. He leans in. She lets him. She touches his arm. If they waltz, I'm done for. Next song — "Slow Dancin'."

Fifty glasses of punch later, the punchbowl is a mound of wet sugar. On the floor, old and new couples clinch. And in the middle, Stephen clings to her. Francis Langley High School. First dance of the year. I'm alone and my bladder hurts.

***

Available from the author - contact Playwrights Union of Canada.

Spring Garden Road

Michael Waller

This confused young man is a sensitive punk rocker in love. He is walking the streets of Halifax to meet with Fiona, the woman of his dreams. On the way he smokes something he shouldn't and falls into a series of very embarrassing mishaps. When he finally sees Fiona, his worst nightmares come true.

HE

It's almost warm tonight. The first time it hasn't been frigid in months. The snow has turned to slush. The slush has turned to mud. Mud is welcomed in Halifax. It's the first sign of spring.

I'm in the little mallette at the corner of Spring Garden and Robie buying smokes. On the other end of the road in an hour I'm going to meet...Fiona. She's the girl I'm going to marry. She doesn't know this. How could she? We just met last week.

I check my hair in the mall mirror. Still sticking straight up. Good. Check my make-up. Still pale. Still smudgy. I look like a corpse. Perfect. I'm ready for the street.

Warm breeze for a change. The kids are out. The irrelevant people have gone home. All the stores are closed. The only things open are bars, restaurants and video arcades. The only people on the street are under thirty.

I turn right and start walking towards Fiona. I'm a little nervous. It is a little nerve-wracking proposing to someone you've only known a week. Still, I know I'm doing the right thing. Besides, I'm sixteen, I'm due for marriage. We've only kissed once. The night we met. Last Wednesday. The perfect kiss. The only problem was my mascara. It smudged on her blouse. Embarrassing.

We haven't kissed since. We've never been alone so how can we express our love for each other? She's been busy; baby-sitting, washing the cat, that sort of thing. For a while it seemed like she might be avoiding me. But tonight she's mine. She's meeting me alone. Alone without her stupid friends to get in the way. This is proof of her love for me.

I light my cigarette in an incredibly cool way and bounce down the street. I've got some time to kill so I sit on a slightly wet bench across from the public gardens and wait for something to happen. And of course nothing does. Typical Halifax. God, this town is so boring. Nothing to do, nowhere to go but home and school and Spring Garden Road. And even Spring Garden Road gets to be a bit of a drag after a while. Luckily, I brought something along to inspire me. It's here in my pocket. One of my debauched friends sold it to me. He even rolled it. One of these days I'll have to learn how to roll a joint. That will be one of my projects for the spring. Right after I learn how to drive.

He lights the joint and begins coughing a lung out.

Hmmmmmm. Smooth.

I go into the Convent of the Sacred Heart. Everyone comes here after they smoke a joint. I don't know why it's so popular. Looking at that big Jesus statue makes me feel a little guilty. Why am I doing this? I didn't even think twice. It must be nerves. Nice though...

I sit on the convent swings for a while and watch the cars go by. Fog is starting to roll in from the harbour and it gives the Public Gardens across the street this really eerie look. Soon they'll open up the gates and, once it's spring, Fiona and I will walk there together, through the flowers. We'll feed the ducks and talk about what we'll name our kids. By that time, me and my band, The Severed Heads, will be famous and Fiona and I will run away from home and we'll get married.

I'm starting to feel a little strange. My hair feels funny. Better make sure it looks okay. I walk further down the street to look for a reflective surface. I get caught by a passer-by fixing my hair in one of the mirrors in front to Spring Garden Place. He snickers as he walks by. Stupid adult. I light another cigarette to calm my nerves. I walk into the Thirsty Duck for a quick beer. I sit down. The room begins to spin.

The benches feel like they have splinters. The colours of the waitresses uniforms fade into one another. What's in this weed? There's a pint of Keith's in front of me, a cigarette lit, I don't know how they got there. I recognize people in the pub. Ex-girlfriends, friends of my mother, ex-French teachers, they're all looking at me, they want to talk to me, they all think my hair looks stupid, does it? Only Fiona knows for sure.

I look at my watch. Time to meet her. Time to get out of this place and straighten up. I run out of the pub. Forgetting to pay.

Smell the salt air. Sound of the music from the bars that line the street. The Clancy Brothers here, Led Zeppelin there. Music from the cars driving by. Kids from Sackville in their Camaros looking for parking. "April Wine at the Metro Centre, Man!" Always a big event in Halifax. I zoom past the library. Past bums sleeping on benches. There's a busker on the library steps playing some Neil Young song. Badly. Kids singing along with him. Really badly. Despite my paranoid state I start to laugh at them and as I laugh I slip in the slushy mud and land at Winston Churchill's feet. The mud's so slippery I have to use his iron legs as leverage. It probably looks obscene. The busker and the kids pause in the middle of "Heart of Gold" and laugh at me. I make it to standing, but my pants are ripped, I'm covered in mud, I'm sure my makeup's ruined, I'm a mess. But I'm almost to Fiona. I walk past the library. The kids are still laughing. Jog down Brunswick Street, I'm at La Cave — our rendezvous point. I look at my watch, I'm only five minutes late, down the stairs into the restaurant. Cheesy music. The waiters look at me wide-eyed. I guess I must be quite a sight. But I must find Fiona. I see her across the restaurant. Serene and beautiful. My future wife. And she's smiling. But she's not smiling at me. She's with people. She's sitting with her parents! Her conservative, respectable, apple-doll manufacturing parents! I've never met these people! I'm stoned, covered in mud, I still look like a corpse and now I have to meet her parents?!

Think quickly. There must be a solution. Men's room. Where is it? Did they see me? Don't look at them. Don't look at them. Found it. Door. Urinal. Stall. Lock. Sit there for ten minutes muttering. This guy comes in, knocks on the stall, I have to get out. This other guy comes in, looks at me funny and I have to pretend to pee, he thinks I'm very strange. Another guy comes in, looks at me, leaves, comes in again, leaves. I think he's very strange.

The longer I spend in this washroom the less able I am to leave. What if her parents saw me? Are they talking about me? What do they think I'm doing in here? What am I doing in here? I'm trapped. I'll be here forever. Is there a window, maybe I can crawl out!

The door opens. God I hope its not that guy again. It's Fiona and she's laughing, "Hey, stupid, what's taking you so long?". And she kisses me — and my mascara smudges on her blouse.

***

Self-contained monologue originally aired on CBC Radio.

Wolfboy

Brad Fraser

Two boys on the verge of manhood try to keep life magical, while coming to grips with the harsh reality of an ugly adult world.

DAVID

When Boots died I wanted to die too. It was like being kicked in the nuts - real hard. I hated him. For giving in to them. For fucking up. I didn't even go to his funeral. His parents blamed me for the whole thing. I went to the theatre instead. Watched The Wolf Man one last time for Boots. I was sitting there — numb — hardly seeing or hearing anything and someone sat down next to me. That's when I realized I was crying. The credits were rolling and I was sitting there with tears all over my face. The person sitting next to me took my hand — held it tight. We got up and left the theatre. Holding hands. I was led to this filthy old boarding house and up a flight of dim stairs. We went into this gray room. I looked up. There was this black guy. With sunglasses on. He was looking at me. It was a full moon that night. I could see it through the window behind him. He reached out and took me in his arms and I cried into his leather. He slipped the collar of my shirt over and bit my neck - bit me hard - till I bled. I remember thinking "Why doesn't this hurt. This should hurt." I felt something moving into me. Something like power. Something like strength. I was seeing things different. He was moving against me and growling. Something exploded in my head and I knew then I'd be all right. I'd make it. Next thing I remember was dressing in the morning to leave. I looked at him laying in the bed watching me leave. He looked so fucking sad.

***

Published by NeWest Press.

My Street

Betty Quan

*East Side Story. In this CBC Morningside radio drama, a
young Chinese-Canadian male, with no trace of an accent,
describes a street in Vancouver's Chinatown. He can mimic his
mother's accent but not in a cruel way.*

NARRATOR

Vancouver. Sunday morning. (*yawns*) Early. After breakfast, Mom and
I go to Chinatown to do the weekly grocery shopping. I park at the lot
at Keefer because street parking is impossible to find. Then, with Mom
ahead and me two steps back, just like the Royal Family, the shop-a-
thon begins.

There's a method to it all, I'm sure there is. The whole routine has to
have a master plan. I mean, every store in Chinatown basically has the
same inventory, right? Wrong, according to Mom. Sure it's got the
same merchandise displayed. Sure the prices are the same, pretty much.
But, Mom sees it all differently: it's like her prescription glasses opened
up a whole new world of comparative shopping and Epicurean
discernment. The best barbequed pork buns here, but the egg custard...
Pender Street; cheapest price for quality oyster sauce; crisper bak choy
there; and more aromatic long grain rice way way way over there; and
fresh carp...(*beat*) Where? We have to go all the way over where?
Mom!?

Mom's first thought is not the week's groceries, but something more
immediate: lunch. And heck, we've just had breakfast! But we might as
well take something home for the rest of the family. And in my family,
we're always thinking about...the next meal. When we eat breakfast, we
think about lunch. When we eat lunch, we think about dinner. Mom
and me — we stop over at Maxim's on Keefer for curried beef,
pineapple custard, and barbequed pork buns.

One box of baked goods. I hold.

Next door has fruits and vegetables: pomelos and pomegranates; papayas and starfruit. Hey Mom, these onions look good, eh? "No. Only fruit good here. We go somewhere else for that."

So we buy a dozen BC reds and two pomelos the size of footballs.

That's one box. Two bags. I hold.

On Gore, the first street east of Main to intersect Keefer, is a shop that sells frozen dim sum. (*calling out like a waiter pushing a dim sum trolley*) *Hargow, sui mai, wo tip.* Hey, Mom, didn't they have these back at Maxim's? "They make it here. Fresher." But they're frozen, Mom. (*beat*) "Fresher frozen. Right here. They make right here. Better. Good."

One box. Three bags. Did you know "fresher frozen" stuff is heavier than nonfresher-frozen stuff? I hold.

From Gore we hit Pender. *Mgoi, mgoi*, excuse me. Excuse me. *Mgoi.* The streets, like any given day, are jammed. I'll accidentally knock unconscious any kid at height with my parcels. We head for mom's favourite butcher shop. There, in the store windows, are whole roast chicken, hanging by their pope's noses, anise-scented duck, and of course barbequed pork, red and sticky and sweet. And in the back room, there's a whole variety of refrigerated meats and poultry. A sensory explosion of the raw and the cooked.

Mom gets some flank steak and a whole seven-pound roasting chicken. She says "I'll carry that. Too heavy by yourself." No, Mom. It's okay. I think my thumb can handle it.

We come upon some of Mom's friends who comment on what a big and strong son she has. And handsome too. Got that right, ladies.

One box. Four bags. One hunched back. I hold, my fingers curling in like mac tacs with the burden of a week's provisions hanging limply off them. We get off Pender and head north on Main to a general goods store so Mom can get some rice vermicelli, peanut oil, watercress and some soya milk. She's lactose intolerant, and I'm bagged.

"Here, I take this and put it in this. Better, heh?" She fits the box of pastries into one of the bags and takes that and the soya milk. It's her one bag against my six. To be fair, she is carrying a purse.

"But wait. We still need onions."
We go backwards, past the butcher on Pender Street, the frozen dim sum shop on Gore, back to Keefer to the place we bought apples and pomelas and where the onions sit. (*slightly sarcastic*) Hey, Mom, I thought you said only the fruit was good here. (*whistles*) And look, the peanut oil's a better price here. "*Ay yah*" is all Mom can say — I don't know what she's ay yahing: the onions, the oil, or, me.

But I'm wrong on all counts. "*Ay yah*. I forget buy the chicken wing." What, Mom? "I forget buy the chicken wing. We go back to butcher shop." But Mom, we can pick up chicken wings from the IGA on the way home. She looks at me for a moment. "What for? Best price on Pender. Best quality. We in Chinatown."

***

Available from author - contact Playwrights Union of Canada.

Strawberry Fields

Michael Hollingsworth

Two young Canadian drifters meet in the aftermath of a rock festival. They find the victim they've been looking for in the form of an American army deserter. Their revenge involves drugs, brutality and other counterculture tactics.

DANNY

You know what happened to me in Salmon Arm, B.C. about four weeks ago? I was about ten miles out of Salmon Arm, B.C. and I'd been trying to hitch-hike all day. And it was raining. And about three o'clock in the morning these two guys came by in a car and said, if I wasn't out of there in twenty minutes they were gonna come back and break both my legs. I got really freaked out. I didn't say anything to them, I just looked at them like this (*making a face*) and they drove away. And I almost started to cry 'cause I was really scared. You know, it was really dark and there was no place to go 'cause it was all hilly and ...I didn't want to go in the bush. And it was cold. But then I started to get really angry. 'Cause I'd been on the road for over eighteen hours and I'd got about thirty miles, half of which I walked. And Salmon Arm is...don't ever get caught in Salmon Arm, B.C. it's a horrible place. I think that, and Hope B.C., and any of the Prairie towns, and of course Wawa, are the infamous places in the world. Anyway, I'm really angry, and I know what I'm gonna do, like I'm not gonna try to talk to these guys, if they come back I'm, you know, I'm gonna get them. So they come back. And the car comes right up level to me. And they roll down the window and the driver says, "I thought we told you..." and the guy on the passenger side opens his door and steps out. And that's when I hit him with my guitar. I went (*demonstrating*) and got him. so he goes back into the car and rolls up the window. And right then it hits me, these guys are nothing. And the feeling of power I had then was so...then I started swearing at the driver to get out of the car, 'cause I knew I had them. And he wouldn't get out. All he did was yell at me, saying he was gonna come back with a couple of clubs and do me in. then he drove off and I never saw them again. I would have liked to have got that driver though, he was a mouthy bastard. but that's what came home to me...I would have killed those guys and drove their car to Calgary or someplace. It was really amazing.

***

Published in "The Factory Lab Anthology" - Talonbooks.

Singing With Ringo

Leslie Mildiner

The monologue, Mouth of the Dragon, is about a young man's childhood in London. He describes a kid's game of 'dare'

LESLIE

With our heads squeezed between the wrought iron railings, eighty feet above the tunnel, Eddie Magee and I stare down at the two giant ventilator fans. A ghostly stream of cars passes silently across to south London, weaving it's way under the Thames. And we are looking into the mouth of a dragon — the hot air taking our breath away. I am dizzy from the car fumes. Then with a quick glance over his shoulder, Eddie is over the gate and racing down the wide, ornate staircase, screaming as he disappears into the darkness — Fearless Eddie, Mad Eddie. I am terrified of going down there, but more afraid of being left on my own, so I follow him. I run down the stairs with my eyes closed, until I catch up with Eddie — clinging to the back of his baggy sweater as he leads us the rest of the way, our feet clanging on the rusting staircase. And suddenly...we're in the tunnel, hot and sweet smelling, cars and buses rushing by inches from our face. Eddie grins: 'Fuckin' all right!' There's a sudden gap in the flow, and Eddie leaps across to the far wall, landing on the pavement barely a foot wide. So we stand in the tunnel, Eddie on one side, me on the other, spread-eagled, pinned against the glistening tiles, dirt and gravel thrown up by passing traffic, stinging our faces...and I think of gun grey metal meeting soft flesh — and I've never felt so alive.

***

Available as a copyscript.

Sunspots

Dennis Foon

*"Sunspots" is the story of five friends, all in their twenties.
Oliver is an uncontrol freak— 'I go where the wind blows me.'
He compulsively steals things, and has a growing collections
of prosthetic arms and legs. He desperately wishes to be a
loyal friend, but can't seem to help sleeping with his best
friend's girlfriend, who is waiting for him in bed as he says
this prayer.*

OLIVER

Brother Andrew used to tell me that You were there, always waiting for
me. All I had to do is let You in. A soothing ointment to cure my
pain.
 A sure hand to guide me through the darkness. and I appreciate that, I
really do, it's a very generous offer. I'll call that Plan B. Because my
understanding is till then anything I do is totally cool with you as long
as I repent at the end and accept You as my savior. which means, I
guess, I'm putting you on hold for now. I realize the main thing is
timing. If I'm hit by a semi or a crashing satellite or fall from K-2 it
means hellfire for sure. I'm playing the odds that something lingering'll
get me and a priest'll be in the vicinity. Plan A.

I try not to sin, I really do. I say to myself, don't do it, don't spit in
that mailbox, don't puke in that guy's convertible, smash that store's
window. You don't need those prosthetic arms of sixteen O Henrys, 12
Bic pens, and that pair of Chinese ringing balls. This week. today.
Because I hate myself when I do it. I truly do. And that's not even the
worst.

Did you see me tonight when I was walking? Checking every bar,
strolling through it, searching for someone to hold. and when there was
nothing, I started to come back here. And I was thinking I don't want to
sin again. God, I don't want to betray my best friend. Stopping at that

department store glass, they've got one of those video monitors on display. And there I am. Smash.

The seven deadly sins. My version. I do nothing with my life: Sloth. I want my best friend's girl: Envy. I take her: Lust. I want he for myself: Greed. Again and again: Gluttony. But no anger. Where's the anger? Why don't I feel anything? Sloth, Envy, Lust, Gluttony, Greed, Sloth, Envy, Lust, Gluttony, Greed.

No anger. No anger. No anger!

***

Available from author - contact Playwrights Union of Canada.

Total Body Washout

Drew Carnwath

A play which charts one man's journey to the edge of modern madness and back again, complete with postcards, x-rays, dreams, and large antlered animals.

JAMES

I do have a crazy aunt — I know, who doesn't right? but this is more than just funny stories at family picnics. Elizabeth. Aunt Ellie. We saw her quite a bit when we were kids — every Christmas and most summers. I can't remember the last time I saw her, because... My clearest memories of Ellie are from those early visits. This one Christmas? Ellie painted all the house plants sparkly red and green, and some of them were gold and silver. I thought it was neat — and kind of weird — but very festive nonetheless, and later I asked Mom why *she* never did cool stuff like that.

I remember the expression on Uncle Pete's face as he tried to make a joke out of it, how 'one of these days I should let Ellie out of the house to get a real job.' But nobody laughed. After dinner my cousin Jodie said that when her Mom ran out of green and red paint she started to use nail polish. 'At least fifty bucks' worth,' Jodie said. That was the first time I realized Aunt Ellie wasn't like most people.

It got worse. Once, when we were invited over for dinner? Uncle Pete came home after work that day to find nothing prepared — Ellie hadn't cooked anything. She'd tried to make a spaghetti sauce but when she filled the pressure cooker with tomatoes it exploded and sent the tomatoes flying all over the kitchen. So! She went out and bought ten tubs of Baskin Robbins Ice Cream because it was Uncle Pete's favorite and she wanted to surprise him. Well. He was surprised. But he never got mad at her. This time he just threw the ice cream out and called Fenton's for catering. And that was the scene in the kitchen when we arrived: Aunt Ellie scraping the hardened tomato off the floor with a letter opener; Uncle Pete tossing whole tubs of Chunky Monkee Ice

Cream into the back yard; and my cousin Jodie standing in between them, crying.

Ellie lives at Ongwanada now. That's a special hospital outside Kingston where families 'deposit' their resident whackos when they become too much trouble. Or too embarrassing. There was never any room for madness in my family. My Grandfather was determined on that point. My Grandmother, too: appearance was everything. If you're gong to go bonkers just do it quietly, dear, and don't tell the Johnsons. Everything will be fine. Pass the watercress, would you, darling? Everything will be fine—

Fucking hypocrites. It's not that easy! My Aunt Ellie had it right! I think she was as sharp as a pin; she was just having fun, fer chrissakes! You want crazy? I'll tell you what crazy is — crazy is living in that house, living *that* life — no life — no *fun*, bored beyond recognition. Talking to those painted plants 'cause they're the only things left for you to love anymore. Nothing left to do but wait...and wait and wait for the day when the waiting can end.

Singing, and fighting tears.

There once was a boy from Berlin
People laughed at his crazy grin
But he didn't care
'Cause they weren't aware
That he lived in a looney bin

Root-a-toot--toot, root-a-toot-toot
I just got out of the institute...

***

Available as a copyscript.

Whale Riding Weather

Bryden MacDonald

*A love story in which a faded old queen, Lyle, who finds his
life slipping away from along with his young lover Auto, who
meets a new, younger man, Jude, and brings him home.*

JUDE

Yeah I saw you in a dream.
I'm sittin in my grandmother's kitchen.
I'm drinkin tea
and the worst thing is happenin:
I'm completely obsessed with how others look at me.
I'm sitting in my grandmother's kitchen
cuz it's the last place I have to go
and I'm completely obsessed with how others look at me.
The only safe place left
and I don't even feel safe there
and that's really weird
cuz I always felt safe in that kitchen.
Then I hear a rumble.
It's a train —
far away like poundin in my ears
and I know it's gonna stop in the kitchen.
I know it's comin for me.
I know it's gonna stop in the kitchen
and there's nothin I can do.
And then it arrives.
Smash.
Right through the wall.
It's an old locomotive
and it's covered with lilacs
because it came through my grandmother's backyard
right through her lilac bushes
and right through the kitchen wall.
And there's nothin I can do.

Hundreds of cars screamin through my grandmother's kitchen
and I can't do a fuckin thing.
Then finally after forever —
it stops.
And you walk out of the last car.

The morning after that dream
my eyes changed colour.

I don't know where I come from
so I can't go back.

Please don't laugh at me.
Do anything
but please don't laugh at me.

What would you do
if I said
I was only on this planet for you
and I'd be content
just to watch you sleep?

***

Published by Talonbooks.

$\mathcal{H}$ouse

Daniel MacIvor

A stand-up / sit-down, comedy nightmare starring Victor. His mother is possessed by the devil, his father is the saddest man in the world. His sister is in love with a dog. The one he loves doesn't love him and he has no place to live.

VICTOR

I'm sitting at Dinny's having my sixth cup of coffee this girl I don't know comes in sits at my booth. She's got a book, she says: mind if I read out loud? I go: WHA? She thinks that's 'yes' she starts reading. After a couple of pages she gets bored and stops. She's looking at me she says: smoking is bad for you. I say: LEAK THAT TO THE MEDIA!

Then we start talking and she tells me about her life and that she's Scottish and then she starts to cry cause she does have a pretty bad life so I play the bagpipes on my throat which is something I do and she likes that cause she's Scottish right. We talk some more and all of a sudden I think, Hey she's a stranger right, a perfect stranger right, perfect.

So I say to her:

'Hey you're a stranger right, a perfect stranger right, perfect. I'm gonna tell you this and ask you something and whatever you tell me I'll go by that.'

So I tell her:

'My mother is possessed by the devil, my father is the saddest man in the world, my sister is in love with a dog, the one I love does not love me and I got no place to live. What should I do?

Now she doesn't jump in with some answers like: 'Join the Y!' No. She THINKS about it. And you can tell that she's thinking about it cause she gets that look of a wrinkled-up forehead and staring off at a spot that isn't there. They are putting the chairs on the tables at Dinny's she's still thinking. We gotta leave, we're walking on the street she's still thinking about it. Walking down by the ravine, she's still thinking. We gotta go back to her place which is this sewer by the highway, well it's more like a tunnel...no, no it's sewer. So we're sitting there in the mouth of her sewer watching trucks go by on the highway she's still thinking about it. Finally the sun's about to come up she gets up walks back to the middle of the sewer looks at me she's got this smile, she's gonna tell me what I should do. But then her smile that she's smiling keeps getting bigger across her whole face and it doesn't stop on her face, it keeps growing and fills up the whole inside of the sewer. Then this smile it turns inside out and from inside the smile walk out all these people: MaryAnn, Millard, Andrew, Doris, my sister, my mother, my father, Darlene, Brenda, Tom, Dave the bishop, people, people, people, all the people I know and they are all wearing this smile of this girl and they are all smiling this smile at me. Then, every one of these people turn into birds. Every different kind of bird. Normal little birds, pigeons, bluebirds, parrots, eagles, birds of extinction, birds from storybooks, every different kind of bird, and then all these birds they come over to me and put their claws in me — but not in my skin! Just in my clothes, in my jacket, in my pants, in my shoes, in my hair a little bit but not too hard...I've got a million wings, and then all these birds they lift me up and fly me right out of the sewer out over the highway over houses over trees over the MOUNTAINS over the OCEAN far far away to this secret field that nobody knows exits — well some people know it but it's very hard to get to — and they drop me down in the middle of this field and I fall asleep and I have this dream:

We're not in the theatre. We're not in the building. We're in this dream. And we're on a bus. Going north. To...Wadawhichawawa. (Wadawhichawawa!) It's very far north and we never been there and that's why we're going. It's night, dark, those little bus lights are on, some people are reading, some people are looking out the window, at the highway going by, trees moving, stars in the moonlight, animal eyes in the woods, dark, quiet. Then that woman at the front, in the blue sweater, the one from the pee break who bought the egg salad sandwich, she starts singing this song and we don't know it but we all start singing it too...well if we sing it I guess we know it...

Well I'm coming by tomorrow with a hacksaw and a hammer
Gonna build a little place for you and me
Be just the way we like it and we'll make sure that it's sturdy
Gonna last a long time for you and me.
And then that sunny morning we will move into our castle
Gonna keep the outside world from you and me
And we'll wake up every morning with our arms around each other and we'll walk into our kitchen and we'll hold our cups of coffee and we'll lookout of our window and how oh so very happy we will be
We will be
and how oh so very happy we will be, be, be
be

***

Published by Coach House Press.

Darkness on the Edge of Town

Eugene Stickland

Four characters, on the Canadian prairie, try to make sense of their lives on the anniversary of the death of a close friend.

TOM

You see, Jason. You find out a lot about yourself playing football. You find out what's going on inside. It's — Christ. I'm afraid I wouldn't know where to begin...

OK, Jason. It's the last game of the regular season. You need to win to get into the play-offs. Your team is down by four points with two minutes left. You need a touchdown. Bad. Don't panic. There's plenty of time. There's not a lot of time, but there's enough time. Now. The fans are sitting in the stands, quiet, sullen. The cheerleaders are standing on the sidelines, their chins on their chests, and their pompoms hanging heavy at their sides. You, Jason, are a wide receiver. In the huddle, the quarterback tells you to run a hook pattern about ten yards out. Nothing too fancy. Nothing too glorious. Not a touchdown or anything. Just a simple first down to keep the drive alive. Are you with me so far, Jason? Good. The ball is snapped. You run down the field, you drive your man to the outside, and cut back into the middle. It's been raining. The field's slick. Your man slips and falls. You're in the open. The QB sees you, sets, and fires the ball. Here it comes. It's coming in high. You're going to have to reach for it, you're going to have to extend yourself, if you want to keep the drive alive, if you want that simple first down. Your man is out of the play. But now that the ball's in the air, you can bet there'll be eleven other guys coming after you like mad dogs. Like pigs. Like mad pigs. The ball's coming in. Where's the safety? Here it comes. Where's the middle linebacker? You reach up and put yourself into your most vulnerable position, stretched out, unprotected, the ball comes in, you squeeze it, you catch it, you got it. And then you hear the footsteps. It's the middle linebacker. He smashes into your left knee with his helmet. Your leg collapses backward. A searing pain shoots up through your body, so hot it takes your breath away. You want to cry. You want to puke. But you hold onto the ball. In that moment of truth, you give your all. Sure, you come down with ripped ligaments. True, you're going to be meat on the table for some half-witted surgeon. Granted, you may never again know the simple pleasure of a stroll around the lake in the evening. But you hold onto the ball. Eventually, as you limp off the field, head high, Jason, head high, you can look into the eyes of the other guys and the coaches, 'cause they know: There goes a guy who's got it. And as you're limping off the field, head high, you notice that the cheerleaders all have tears in their eyes because they understand, and their thighs itch because they see, limping before them, A MAN. A man. And it's not always easy, being a man.

***

Available as a copyscript.

Honeyman

Andrew Akman

*"The Train Crash" In this speech, the actor describes the event
which made him realize he was an invincible protector of the
weak and innocent; a superhero called The Phoenix.*

ANDREW

As a small child I lived unaware of my true nature, unsuspecting of the
legacy I bore. Happy was my life as Little Atom Andy. But then, one
dark and snowy night, at the age of seven, something happened which
would change my life forever. Every Sunday night, before my parents
separated, we had family dinner at Grammy Sadie and Saboo Sam's; my
Mom's parents. Sadie would cook up some kind of pineapple chicken
something. She'd feed us that and a bowl of salad dressing with a little
bit of lettuce in it and always, always homemade rhubarb tapioca pie for
dessert. Saboo Sam has always tolerated Sadie's cooking. He's a
tolerant, thin man. The night Sam politely declined to eat a piece of
Sadie's infamous tapioca pie with a trace of rhubarb in it, the marriage
almost ended. All he said was; "No thanks Sadie, I'll pass on the
rhubarb pie." And a fifty-year relationship hung in the balance. Saboo
Sam suggested we go to Dairy Queen for dessert instead. "But Saaaam,
it's winter, it's cold out." "So *nu*, it's Winnipeg." We all pile into the
station wagon to drive to Dairy Queen. And the snow is coming down.

In the front we've got Dad driving, Mom in the middle, Saboo Sam on
the passenger side. In the back it's me, my little sister Justine, my
brother Matthew and Grammy Sadie on the passenger side. My littlest
sister Gwyn isn't born yet. And for just a second I wonder why Justine
isn't on my Mom's lap like every other night. Why tonight? And of all
the dessert places we could have gone to in the North End, why are we
crossing the train tracks to the South End? Why Dairy Queen? And as
my father crosses the tracks, my grandparents look up through their
passenger windows into a big white light.
The train begins to mulch the car under its engine. In another five
seconds we will be crushed to death but the tail end of the wagon hits a

Manitoba Hydro pole which swings us off the tracks into the ditch. When the car stops, my Dad looks around. His wife is doubled over moaning from some unknown internal injury. His in-laws are slumped over bleeding from their heads trapped in a tangle of metal. He calls out to his three children and there is no answer.

He is twenty eight years old, the age I am now. It's possible he's just killed his wife, her father, her mother, and his three children. He opens his door and jumps out of the car. He collapses on his ankle which has been shattered in the crash. He rips open the back door and finds his three kids on the floor in a pile. I'm on the bottom. Justine's in the middle and Matthew's lounging on the top. His nose is gushing blood but he's got an ear to ear grin. He though the ride was fun. He wants to do it again. And Justine's smiling too because in the moment before impact I wrapped her in my arms — for sure her little neck would have snapped without me. And if she had been on my Mom's lap like every other night, she would have sailed through the windshield. But on this night, I protected her. I wrapped her in my wings and saved her life.

Grammy Sadie and Saboo Sam eventually come to. Sadie pries open one blood-caked eyelash and gives Sam a little wink. And Sam tries to reach around to kiss her but he can't because he still wrapped in metal. So he whispers to his wife of fifty years, "Sadie, next Sunday we eat rhubarb pie."

Score cards read: Saboo Sam — broken ribs, punctured lung, loss of hearing in right ear. Grammy Sadie — broken ribs, fractured skull, loss of vision in right eye. My mother's got broken ribs and a ruptured spleen. My father's in physiotherapy for a year. Matthew's got a broken nose. But Justine and I walked away without a scratch. For seven years my powers had lain dormant. But they were re-ignited in the fire of the train crash. On the way to Dairy Queen, for a Peanut Buster Parfait, I discover I am the invincible protector of the weak and innocent.

***

Available from author - contact Playwrights Union of Canada.

The Story of a Sinking Man

Morris Panych

Nash inexplicably finds himself sinking into a bog with no way out — he is distinctly alone. He reviews his predicament and his life but doesn't give up hope of rescue.

> *NASH is up to his ankles in mud. As he struggles, he sinks a little further down into it.*

NASH

Oh, dear. Don't move — don't panic. Stay calm.

> *He stands for another long time, looking out.*

(*calling*) Who sees me? Anybody? Hasn't anybody seen me, yet!? (*looking around*) I'd been like this for hours. He said. He did? Yes. Later. At the press conference. Following his...ordeal. He spoke of his amazing rescue. As they all...took notes. He...told them how he'd been stuck for hours, in the mud. And how nobody came. Nobody came, they asked. A bird. He told them. Just a bird, he told them, sitting on a branch, came along to have a look at me. Who else *would* come? Well, there must have been somebody who would have noticed you were missing. Yes. But how would they know I was in *this* situation? Who would guess? When something happens to someone, you don't automatically assume mud is involved. Not unless you're a journalist...gentleman. Ladies. I tried not to panic. That's the thing. I just waited quietly for someone to come along, and talked...to the wind. He told them. And waited. I could count, I thought, But then...count to what? When would I know I was at the end of counting? Those were the kinds of things that went through my mind. Another question? My life? Oh, yes. I thought about that a lot. When I was a child, I would always imagine myself falling through a hole in the ice. From beneath, I could see the warped images of people walking about. Even trees and birds, but I couldn't break through to them, so I would drown. That must have been very unpleasant for you. Well, in a way it gave me a perspective on the world. A sort of view from below. Later in life it would help me to cope with things like departments of civic planning, applications for bank loans. Questionnaires. That sort of...thing. So you're saying that even bad situations can become positive ones. Well, yes. I think so. I mean, there I was, stuck in a puddle. The setting sun about to leave me...standing, alone, in the dark. I had to consider what good might come of that.

> *And so he waits, expectantly, as the sun goes down.*

So the whole night through, I kept watch over myself, as if I were my own guardian angel.

With morning came renewed hope, that a stranger would come along to offer me assistance. And so I waited. Suddenly a little bug landed, nearby. Hello, little friend. Are you looking at me? Perhaps you're wondering what I'm doing here. Are you? Let me explain. It's very simple. Without realizing what I was stepping in...but you seem to be sinking a little yourself. Are you stuck? Oh, dear, your wings are all heavy now, aren't they? You won't be able to fly like that, will you? You'll just sink into oblivion, with no one the wiser. Unless someone pulls you out of this mess. But who? What if no other bug passes by and sees you? You'll just have to pray to God, won't you? Hoping that he exists in this one instance. After all, he was invented for situations like these. Where is he now? Are you praying, little bug? I hope you've said your prayers. Oh, look. Here he comes. Here comes the hand of God to lift you up out of the miserable, sinking world you've landed yourself in. (*reaching down*) Oh. (*falling silent for a moment*) I couldn't quite...if I'd gone any further...It was a question of whose life was worth saving, I thought to myself. I tried to put the little death out of my mind. But I would never forget the image of those sad bug eyes looking at me...helplessly...as the tiny thing disappeared...out of sight.

> *He considers the bug's fate, then looks out into the distance, considering his own.*

***

Published by Playwrights Canada Press in
"Singular Voices - Plays in Monologue Form".

The Last Adam

Vittorio Rossi

*A play about the Leones, a Montreal "family" and their
"business" which is organized crime. Salvatore is the second
son, 29, and a drifter. Here he is talking to his older brother
Marco.*

SALVATORE

I was waiting. I go for my second cup. He starts with that snickering.
Like some superior attitude. What does he care? I'm paying the coffee.
And what, I won't leave him a tip? Then I go for a third cup, and all the
while I'm ordering in French. Then, of course, he starts to pretend he
don't understand me. Like I'm a foreigner or something. *I was fucking
born here!* First they throw the French language down your throat, and
then when you speak it, they criticize the manner in which you talk. I
go on to my fourth cup of coffee. Now I'm thinking, okay, maybe he's
insulted by my French, so let's talk English. He responds in French. So
this is a no-win situation. He thinks I can't win this one. I'm the
customer. I'm the one who's paying. Where's the courtesy? Let me tell
you, there is none. These fucking frogs want to bust my ass. I say fuck
you. There's what....five million of them? I'll take 'em all on. They
wanna push us all outta here. Go ahead! See what happens to this place:
fucking Third World. That's what. And you don't think it's possible?
Culture? that's what they call it? A culture that is threatened by the
word STOP. *An international fucking word.* Nowhere it's a problem.
but here it's a catastrophe. Here they have studies that finally said
STOP is a legal word. Isn't that so fucking brilliant!

I ordered my fifth cup. Now I'm thinking, well you're not showing up,
something came up. So as he fills up my cup, I ask for the check.
"Quoi?" he says, like some fucking duck. So I leave my money on the
table. With tip.

He's walking back towards the cash register which is near the door. so
as I open to leave I bring him out with me. I told him, 'Listen *Paesano*,

I'm Italian and you just fucked with the wrong person.' Bing. I popped him one. He goes down like a fucking fairy. The manager comes running out, I say, 'You just remember who my forefathers were. I'm a connected guy. I'll have you shut down in a minute.' and I left.

Now. You wanna talk about the future.

***

Published by NuAge Editions.

Scheme-a-Dream Christmas

Caroline Russell-King

It's Christmas Eve in a balloon-a-gram office. The clown, Fifi the maid, Santa, an ape, and an elf resolve their conflicts, trapped in an office with no power or telephones.

GEORGE

In elementary school, I was the only Jewish kid. It was great except for Spike, the school bully. One year we had to put on the Christmas concert. I was singing carols for three weeks of rehearsals, but on the night, the teacher decided I should open with a solo. In the front row sat my mother, father, Baba and Zeda. And here I was standing on stage in front of a nativity scene. I took a deep breath and began "God rest you merry, gentlemen, let nothing you dismay. Remember um our um um um was born on Christmas day." Children started to snicker, I started to cry. Spike, who was playing a shepherd, decided to take matters into his own hands. He hit me over the head with his shepherd's crook. It worked, I stopped crying, but then I got mad, really mad. I wanted to hit him back. I didn't have a weapon. I picked up the nearest thing available. The doll in the manger. I hit Spike over the head with the baby Jesus. When I picked up the doll there was a collective gasp from the audience. The whole production went downhill from then on. Spike and I started circling each other, he was jabbing with his staff, I was swinging the doll. Spike jabbed, I ducked, and one of the kings got it right in the stomach. He keeled over and the other two kings threw down their crowns and rolled up their sleeves. And I guess that was when the fight officially broke out. The teacher was busy trying to close the curtain. The girl playing Mary started to scream at me to put down the baby. It was her doll. The set fell down just before the curtain closed and that was my first and last Christmas concert.

***

Available as a copyscript.

The League of Nathans

Jason Sherman

*Nathan Isaacs, 30, has come to Spain with his old friend
Nathan Abramowitz to meet a third friend from childhood,
Nathan Glass. While they wait at the appointed place for the
rendezvous, Isaacs appeals to Abramowitz for spiritual
guidance, and discovers that Abramowitz has abandoned his
faith.*

ISAACS

What about your bar mitzvah, didn't you cry at your bar mitzvah? I
think I remember you cried at your bar mitzvah...you don't remember
that? I mean that took balls, Nathan. That took balls, to stand up there
and weep. Nathan: what do you suppose happens to a Jew when he
dies? Like heaven and hell, Jew heaven and Jew hell, I mean where are
they? What are they? I never could figure that out. Where do you go?
What happens if you're not good. This is something you know. You
always knew this shit. When we were growing up, you were always
talking about God, you were always like Mister Mystic. That time in
the field, you remember that, when we saw that light, and you said it
was a light from God, remember that? I thought that was bullshit, but I
thought about it, it never left my mind. It stayed with me, it crawled
right inside me. And then when I got the telegram, it fuckin' floored
me, I just about dropped dead, yeah, because not two days earlier was
Yom Kippur, and my little conversation with the Rabbi. I mean I told
you I had this conversation about trying to be better, trying to do
better. You think it just came to me like that? Rabbi Mandelbrot gave a
little talk I never heard a talk like this. He started off by saying he was
leaving the synagogue, he was quitting being a Rabbi. I mean we're
stunned. The shul is packed like I said, it's Yom Kippur. He says he's
been thinking about it a long time, and he's come to the realization that
Israel being the way it is, he cannot in all good conscience continue to
be a Rabbi. "In all good conscience." That's what he said. He said you
can't have both a Jewish state and a Jewish religion. Then he told us
why. He gave us like this whole history of Israel, Nathan, a history we

don't get. I'm telling you it made me sick. You can't tell me the guy could make up a history filled with so much, so much—.

Mandelbrot, he, right in front of the congregation, he took off his tallis, laid it over the Torah. Then he walked out, right up the centre aisle. Total fuckin' silence. Can you imagine? Jesus. I called him up the next day, went over to see him in his little apartment. He was packin' up. Getting ready to move to Israel. I said, "After what you just said in the shul?" He goes, "I'm going to make sure the Jews stay Jewish." Then he dug out this scrapbook, all kinds of pictures he's been keeping of shit happening in Israel. Had this whole section on Lebanon, Beirut blown to shit, refugee camps, the whole thing. And this one picture, of a little girl, couldn'ta been more than four. A fuckin' angel, with these huge eyes, just this perfect little girl. Then I saw her leg was in a cast. It was in a cast because a bomb tore her foot off. A bomb knocked her house down. A bomb killed her family. An Israeli bomb. A Jewish bomb.

Then two days later I'm holding the telegram from Glass. I thought to myself, I need this and out of nowhere, from somewhere inside me, came this memory about the light, about that time you saw heaven, and I knew, Nathan can tell me about heaven, he can help me get to heaven...You cried at your bar mitzvah. Hey. You cried at your bar mitzvah...What the hell happened to you?...You used to be this—

I hate to see that. A guy's got certain things he believes, he pisses them away, forgets about 'em, bullshit. You, Nathan, you had some kind of belief. Now you tell me you don't believe — I mean what the fuck? Did you give up, what? How do you account for that? Listen to me. I'm talking about right now. I'm saying you've got people, you've got friends, you've got one chance to get on side before the world starts expecting things out of you, you've got this much time to be the thing you most want to be, and the rest of it you're convincing yourself that's what you became. I know what I am, Nathan. You think this is it? You think I sleep nights? You think I don't get up ten times a night and look at myself in the mirror. I look at myself, Nathan, I ask myself what I see. I don't see a fucking thing. Shit, Nathan. I'm asking you for help. I'm asking you to help me.

***

Available as a copyscript.

Falling Back Home

Sean Dixon

A man, in his early thirties, tells his 11-year-old son about the mother the boy has never met.

YOUNG JOSEPH

I first met Molly on a...well, everybody's got one of these stories, though I suppose you don't, but you will, maybe, where you're sitting on a streetcar in the Big City, and this woman gets on, say, or this man I suppose, but I'm going to talk about a woman. She gets on and takes a seat in front of you and to the left, and since you're both facing front you can't really see her face, only you get the impression that she's looking at you out of the corner of her eye. And just when you think you're kidding yourself, this woman hasn't been sent by God to answer all your prayers and dreams, she turns all the way around in her seat, looks you straight in the eye and smiles. She smiles at you like she knows you, like you had met her somewhere before and are connected somehow. And her smile starts to go just as yours begins, because you're a second or two behind, being in complete shock and all. But that's enough to skewer the moment and turn her around in her seat again to face front and open the window with a thump. Boy when that window went thump I could've just died. And then a bit of time goes by when you realize you haven't really been breathing, and then you start breathing again and you start to ask yourself why why why why? Why did she smile at me? And what does she want me to do about it? And you wonder should I ask her "Excuse me, do you know me? You smiled as if you knew me." And then you start to imagine yourself asking that question, and, even though it's easy enough to imagine, you realize that you just don't have the strength to accomplish it. Ain't it the truth.

The only thing you can hope is that the streetcar will get to Yonge, since you've already passed University going east and she didn't get off there, the streetcar will get to Yonge and the car will empty out completely but she won't get off and since it's just you and her left it would be absolutely absurd for you to not say anything under the circumstances. And then for a moment you think that's the way it's going to be, since she's one of those really level people who wait till the last possible second before she gets up and gets off, at Yonge. So that's it.

But it goes even further, because you get up and get off after her even though it's just about too late, so it's obvious, but instead of going down the subway stairs behind her you panic and continue walking east on King or whatever for about ten feet, before you turn around and see her just hesitating at the top of the stairs. And then starts down. Damnit. Damnit. Fucking hell it's true, it's so clear, don't use this kind of language. The point is it wasn't my imagination...but you think it's clearly too late now, which it's not, and you realize that two blocks later when it really is too late. But you go back anyway and pay the fare just to get on the subway platform, but she's not there. This scenario can go on for weeks: You could choose to ride the streetcar at the same time from the same place every day for days and days and days, but it's a Big City and blah blah blah. But that's what I did, and that's how I finally met Molly.

Molly wasn't the girl who had smiled at me the first time, so technically she wasn't the woman I was looking for. She was somebody else, who got on the streetcar at the same time every day just after I did, and sat in the same place that the original woman sat in, just in front of me and to the left, unless it was taken, which was rare. This went on for three weeks and two days, not including weekends, before I finally spoke to her.

***

Available from author - contact Playwrights Union of Canada.

Ilsa, Queen of the Nazi Love Camp

Blake Brooker

A nasty musical comedy satire on intolerance, paranoia, and denial of The Holocaust.

JIM KEEGSTRA

There's a few things in life a man can count on.
Really count on.
The internal combustion engine is one of them.

With a manual in his hand now.

Each part has a purpose.
Each part needs the other parts to fulfill their purposes in order to fulfill its own.
When that happens the thing moves.
Forward or backward, depending on the gear shift.
I don't care whether it's a tractor, a truck or a train.
When each part does its job, the thing moves.
The truck backs up to the loading dock.
The train hauls its load into the night.
The tractor plants wheat that makes bread for the cities.
In an engine there's no such thing as a part without a purpose.
No single piece without a function. It wouldn't make sense.
To attach a part that does nothing to an engine that does something,
namely move, is wasteful stupidity.
A waste of effort.
From Bible study we all know the story of Onan.
Onan and his first epistle.
Onan in the wilderness alone.
Just him and his epistle, waiting in the desert.
And yes, it came to pass.
Onan spilled his seed on the dry earth.
By himself.

A dissipation, a leakage if you will, that dripped into the barren soil and served no purpose.
A wasteful stupidity.
Like a part that does absolutely nothing while it's attached to an engine that's doing all the hard work.
The useless part is what I call a Technological Onanism.
A wasteful thing, to no good purpose.
(*joking*) Like a pickle tied to a cowboy hat.

(*becoming serious again*) A passenger, a freeloading rider being carried along, getting fat on the work of others.
That condition just does not exist
in internal combustion engines.
That is why I trust them.
Why I can count on them.
They inspire me.
I'll take a look at your car. Go for a ride around the block.
Sneak a look under the hood.
Chances are there's nothing wrong.
But if there is — a couple of calls to the auto wreckers and a night in my garage, she'll be as good as new.

(*pause*) Cash only. Sorry.

(*remembering something painful*)

I don't believe in credit. And no cheques.
Banks and I...well you know.
You might say society is like an internal combustion engine.
Each of us a single part, yet each of us depending on the others and all of us moving together.
But if you think about it, and I don't believe you need any special qualifications, I mean I know I'm a mechanic, and it's easy for me to understand, but I think a Christian can follow this too —
Anyways, if you think of society as an engine, and we're all parts, then look at yourself.
What's your function?
Are you a spark plug, say, or a hose?

If we look at society as an engine, then it doesn't take a mechanic or a Christian to figure out that [*looking skyward*] we'd better call the garage and make an appointment real fast.

(*pause*) And don't even think of using a credit card.

(*with a big smile*) There's no banks up there.

(*pause*) Lots of parts in this engine don't seem to fit.
Don't have a clear purpose.
Lots of parts seem to be along for the ride.

You know I've had a little trouble.
I thought I was part of the motor.
I felt good. I felt strong. I didn't ride. I did my job.
I taught school, participated in politics.
I've always been community minded.
A good neighbour.
I believed young people are the building blocks of our nation, and I worked hard for my position.
What's your position?
Are you a fly wheel or a gas tank?
Me, it's hard to remember what I was, but now some people call me a crankshaft.

(*looking into the audience*) Who are the riders?

Who's the muffler?

***

Published by Red Deer College Press.

The Tyrant of Pontus

Thomas Coyle

A tragi-comedy about the family life of the King Mithridates Eupator, achieves surreal textures through a blend of highly-wrought verse with vivid contemporary prose. Here the choric Messenger practices a speech to be delivered to the king's treacherous son, Pharnakes, relaying the 'bad' news that, despite the prince's best efforts, his father has survived that day's battle against the Romans under Pompey the Great.

MESSENGER

From strife fast I speed me here—
Full gauged of woe — to tell my tale
Lord Pharnakes all that's lost.

Ten times' terrors these times rend;
And I quake to give them sound.
Let me pause to shape my theme.

This street will be the palace.
Black rats can for viz'ers stand.
Bits of bones will be my Lord.

Post haste will I be let in;
And, so bowing to all there,
Pronounce in tones of sorrow:

"Prince, son of Mithridates:
From Eupator greetings come!"
Stop. That's how to lose a head.

Pharnakes hates his Father,
And would take his Father's place;
And he, for his Father's ruin,

Planned with Pompeius to leave
The field for Rome's advantage.
I must strike a higher pitch.

Good Lord: in Fortune's heart are we held not,
And so do struggle now in deepest dark
With Luck and Valour gone howling from us!
In vain — in vain! — we fought while Life and Breath
Ran out all resistless to foreign arms.
Our corps, thus daggered by Romantic thrust,
Spun giddy: above, an eclipse of spears;
Below, a turmoil of unaugured guts
So slicked the ground that those not fallen fell;
On all sides, an Italic host made mad
To spill the blood of sweet Caucasian youth!
Then did Great Pompey order forth his horse,
Which, with ten-thousandfold thunder's pounding,
Shook the World, and charged foaming to slaughter.
Amazed, we ran; while they, laughing, let us;
For by our confusion was their mirth increased.
So with cruel clemency did some escape
The field of danger. In shame, am I of those.
Thus in one day is all Asia undone:
Our Mother lies harlot to Rome's desires!
I'm sent to tell you this: Eupator lives.
O Prince! — I've myself no voice to command,
Except as your good Father's forerunner—
You're bid to welcome King Mithridates,
Who follows hard on me, your humblest slave.

Put thus, I might stay intact.
The bad news will please him,
Erecting his penependent
Plot to such high swollen heights
That, when falls the house of good
News, he, shrivelling, may me neglect!

Then, bowing once (or twice), I'll take my leave of Prince, King,
Kingdom; all;

And— Thanks be to the Lord of Light! — to some far distant safe place run!
Although a part of me (strange thought!) — would even pay to see the fun.

***

Available from the author - contact Playwrights Union of Canada.

Saint Sebastian

Bruce Bell

*A play about love, jealousy, death and running a theatre
company in Heaven.*

BRIAN

When I first arrived in Heaven, after my brutal, yet highly publicized
murder at the hands of my slightly demented lover Sebastian, I
immediately went searching for a basic and fundamental question. Does
God actually speak to people — specifically those who have a "Holier-
than-thou" attitude about their place in the Universe? Sebastian...
beautiful, tragic Sebastian...terribly mixed up, as only those who were
raised on *Leave it to Beaver* while being shuffled from foster home to
foster home can be, never once spoke of God until...

...When I first met him I had just lost my job writing witty responses
for Finnegan, to Casey's archaic ideologies on *The Mr. Dressup Show*.
I was fired when I suggested we all should go vogueing at Colby's. Do
you realize how many of today's top drag queens were first inspired by
Mr. Dressup? Mind you, I enjoyed working at the CBC, but being dead,
as I am now, I can reflect that those days were wasted. I always thought
being dead and working for the CBC were one and the same... Being
dead is far more fulfilling.

When I entered Heaven I was asked, by a woman who handed me a
martini, if I would like to take over the running of Heaven's National
Theatre, "The Theatre of the Dead". The company had been floundering
for an eternity doing *Hedda Gabler* and would continue to do so until
Henrik Ibsen showed up and told them to stop. I accepted the job, we're
still waiting. In the meantime, I'm workshopping a new play I have
written with the hope of producing it — if and when *Hedda* ever closes.
It's the story of my last days on earth, leading up to my murder. It's
called St. Sebastian - The Ultimate Passion. I've asked Rupert, one of
the members of my young company, "Artists-who-don't-require-
Government-assistance-'cause-they're-dead Theatre Ensemble," to play

Sebastian. You'll have to excuse Rupert. I think he's still in love with me. We dated for a while up here. Fifty years? I really can't remember. Anyway, he's pissed off because I won't write a play about him...I could only write for Sebastian. My last ten years on earth were either for, about or starring Sebastian. He acted in four of them...Oh, he was good. He could have gone on but...Rupert here doesn't understand. I don't want to make the same mistakes.

So that morning, down at the Morrissey, me drinking my coffee and him slugging back his beer, has remained the singular most cherished memory I have of Sebastian. He was so charming, so witty, so informed about the world surrounding us...He was also drunk and passed out by 3 in the afternoon. I dragged him to the curb, threw him into a cab and took him back to my place I managed to get him up the stairs and into my apartment. Then the little angel threw up... in the bathroom... not in the toilet, but the bathroom none the less. He staggered out and fell on my bed and went to sleep. I stood over him and watched this sleeping beauty for the longest time. Then I got onto the bed with him.

Sebastian and I spent our first night together lying in my bed, drinking gin, smoking cigarettes and me listening to the stories of how he got his tattoos. Sometimes when he was babbling on about something I could care less about, like baseball, I would just like stare at his face. Not listening to a word he was saying but pretending to. Was I wrong? As far as he knew, I was listening. I remember feeling alive for the first time in my life. Had I not met Sebastian, I never would have known the feeling, and being dead, like I am now, would not be an experience, would it?

***

Available as a copyscript.

Through the Eyes

Don Druick

*Paris, 1665, and the danger and opulence of the French court.
The great Italian artist, Gianlorenzo Bernini, comes to France
to carve a portrait of the Sun King.*

COURTIER

There is an incident at Fountainbleu. Our master Louis is hunting, is it
the falcons or the hounds? And, and we with him. It is beautiful
beautiful and early spring day, how I love these days, the buds the air,
crisp and clear so clear. One feels for a moment one can really see. We
are all in fine fettle, the gentlemen of the court, despite having been up
oh so late the night before tasting of the sparkling local vintage. that
night, how we did laugh, the King at his wittiest as we sang the old
songs of François Villon. So wonderful to remember this soulful
melody. And why? And especially now? Can it be that it is like my
childhood?

So as is said, we are hunting but we can find no worthy prey. No
brocket no boar nor stag. It is the nature of the game but nothing
worthy nothing banal nothing nothing at all. We search and search we
ride but nothing absolutely nothing. After a long while of this, mon
Louis, the mirror of all our souls, turns suddenly to his Master of the
Hunt, his father's Master of the Hunt, Pierre Claude-Marie LaRoche.

(*as LOUIS*)	And so, Monsieur LaRoche?
(*as LAROCHE*)	M'Lord?
(*as LOUIS*)	And so?
(*as LAROCHE*)	M'Lord?
(*as LOUIS*)	There is nothing, Monsieur LaRoche. What are we to imagine?
(*as LAROCHE*)	Je suis désolé, M'Lord, but what can one do?
(*as LOUIS*)	Is that it then?
(*as LAROCHE*)	M'Lord?

| (*as LOUIS*) | Is that it? Would you have done so little for my father? |
| (*as LAROCHE*) | Old King Louis, m'Lord? |

We laugh at poor Pierre's plight. I decide then and there I will give him a bottle of my finest cognac when the day is done. We laugh but something, how shall I convey this, in the King's tone quickly sobers us. Mon Louis, our heartbeat, hesitates. The Marquis de Bellefonds, the King's left hand, the Minister of Culture, and perhaps it is rumoured, the Fifth Musketeer, whispers in the royal ear.

(*as BELLEFONDS*)	What say you, Sire, should not this LaRoche be our prey?
(*as LOUIS*)	Ah. (*pause*) Yes. So be it.
(*as LAROCHE*)	I do not understand, m'Lord.
(*as BELLEFONDS*)	Be as a little animal. Go. Run. Scamper.
(*as LAROCHE*)	M'Lord?

Monsieur LaRoche is shivering in the morning cold.

| (*as LOUIS*) | Be off. (*pause*) Now. |
| (*as BELLEFONDS*) | And without your horse. |

In the silence, a bird, suddenly so large, flies across the sky. Pierre turns and runs. We look to the King.

| (*as LOUIS*) | Give him five, no ten minutes, and then we pursue. We will have meat for the table tonight, eh? |

The laughter that follows is dry, and quickly disappears into the landscape. The silence is long.

| (*as LOUIS*) | (*pause*) Now. Loose the hounds. We ride. Which way? Which way? Yes. There he is. Towards the palace. |

LaRoche is almost at the gates. Mon Louis, the regal Louis laughs. the Marquis de Bellefonds cannot resist the opportunity to shout.

| (*as BELLEFONDS*) | He is looking for abed to hide under. |

(*as LOUIS*) A bag of gold to the man who kills the game.

We enter the palace itself, horses hounds harriers. An awesome sight. Inside the palace inside the very palace. A roar like I have never heard before. By now LaRoche has climbed the grand marble staircase magnificent glistening pure white, the heartbeat of the palace, broad and sweeping up and up and up till it almost touches sweet heaven itself. Our Louis the sailor of all the oceans, charges the staircase his horse slipping and cracking on the marble. Most follow the King, but I...stay behind. The smell in the air is blood.

(*as LOUIS*) Flourish the mort. Flourish the mort.

The roar the racket a symphony of death. The devil's hounds do howl. LaRoche is almost at the top when the first rider, the chevalier de Nogent, the youngest son of the legendary Prince de Condé, splendid in a blue damask jacket splendid upon a regal white stallion reaches him passes him rears above him. the moment is sublime: white horse white marble white eyes. Forever. Suddenly with a swift oh so swift swift motion, the Chevalier de Nogent reaches down with his dagger and cuts Pierre's throat one side to the other. Blood everywhere now the marble alive with colour. Blue jacket white horse red blood. Pierre Claude-Marie LaRoche with a gaggled cry slowly crumbling jerking painfully spasmodically arms legs flailing as he falls tumbling slowly down down down down down accelerating now more and faster faster again and coming to a rest just two stairs from the bottom. Almost in front of me. At moments like this, I pray: "oh Lord, please grant me just one more day on this earth."

(*as LOUIS*) Well there it is.

LaRoche's eyes remain open.

It is our sacred tradition that the royal family may never sleep, will never sleep in a house where someone has died. So the Marquis de Bellefonds drags the perhaps and barely alive Pierre Claude-Marie LaRoche, a trail of blood, to die alone in the darkening mist of the courtyard. I think of Isabelle, his wife of so many years. I silently vow to never hunt again. I know I will drink that bottle of my finest cognac when the day is done.

***

Available as a copyscript.

Elvis & Mavis

Jeff Pitcher

An unemployed Newfoundlander sits atop the Churchill Falls
Hydro Dam and threatens to blow it up unless the contract
between Newfoundland and Quebec for rights is renegotiated.
His wife sits at home trying to figure out what went wrong.
Was it something she said?

ELVIS

I think Newfoundland is finished. She's at rock bottom, b'y. Oh, I knows there's lot that thinks it but I knows it. I'm not even one of your statistics anymore. Used to be but since me unemployment run out I'm nudding no more. Not even a blip. I'm from Sin John's, eh, but I lives in Roddickton but that's not where I am now. Laberdor. That's all I can tell ya. All I knows is we're stunned. Newfoundlanders! From John Crosbie to Gordon Pinsent, we're all as stunned as yer arse. 500,000 stunned-arsed arse holes tryin' to make a go of it on a bald rock in the middle of the Atlantic — no, I knows you're not stunned. I mean, what were they thinkin'? Our forefadders? Why in the name a' Jesus did they have to stop here for? All they had to do was travel on for another day or two and we would've all been raised in the nice, lush, beautiful Annapolis Valley of Nova Scotia or the lovely protected island of Prince Edward wit' d'ere sandy beaches, good weadder an' Canadian Forces bases. But, no, they had to pick the first place they laid eyes on where it's winter for 10 mont's a' d'e year. A place where d'ere's hardly a spot to pitch a house 'cept the side of a cliff. I mean, what was wrong 'em? They didn't wanna deal wit' the hardship a' sailin' on up the St. Lawrence to Quebec, the most profitable country in d'e country. No, our forefadders had to take the easy way out an' enjoy the serene life of settlin' in the only Third World country in the western world! (*beat*) That is my point. We're stunned! And I'm gonna do somethin' about it. I'm gonna blow it up.
No, I'm not gonna blow up Newfoundland. Just part of it. The Churchill Falls part. That's where I am now. (*smiling*) The whole thing. The falls, river, dam. Why? 'Cause I'm pissed off, that's why. Is

there anything not to be pissed off about? (*beat*) Well, that's the first thing, you know. My name. Elvis. I mean all my life I've had to live with that handle, you know. Elvis. Elvis Parsons. I mean, I'll never know why Mom called me that, you know. It hasn't been easy. Bein' called Elvis all your life is a lot like bein' a Newfoundlander, you know. I mean, I can change my name or a Newfoundlander can go away but I'm still gonna be Elvis and a Newfoundlander is gonna be a Newfoundlander no matter where he is. (*beat*) I am not stunned! I mean, I am stunned as a Newfoundlander but I am not stunned as me! I knows exactly what I'm doin'. I got a hundred sticks a' dynamite stuffed around strategic places all over the dam an' power house an' with one single finger I'll have the whole system blowed right out including electric power all over Newfoundland, Montreal, half a' New York State plus the Big Apple itself. (*beat*) Whenever I feels the time is right. I'm just lettin' the people a' Newfoundland know what's goin' on before I does it. (*beat*) Oh, an' just one odder t'ing. I'd just like to apologize to the feller I bought the ski-doo from in Churchill Falls. The cheque's gonna bounce. Oh, you'll never find me — don't have to believe me if ya don't want to, but then again, if ya believed in Joe Smallwood, I daresay you'll believe anyt'ing! See ya!

***

Available as a copyscript.

L'Affaire Tartuffe

Marianne Ackerman

"Or The Garrison Officers Rehearse Molière." A young director wants to explore an odd historical incident from 1774. When a power failure suddenly plunges the dinner party into darkness, the candles come out and the scene segues seamlessly into the historical action of the director's script. The character Fraser is the host of the party in the modern setting and an ex-British Army officer in the past setting. Here he describes the death of his father during the battle of Culloden, between Scottish clansmen and England.

FRASER

April 16, 1746, sunrise. My father went off to a fight, left me with my mother to guard the house. I was nine years old. All day, we could hear the wounded as they passed, cursing the Redcoats, cursing each other, pounding on the door.

Cries of agony as they staggered home to die. The wicked stench of blood and smoke.

Sometime in the night came a knock at the door.

Two men, called out my name.

We let them in...

They told us how my father died.

The field was thick with the blood of Fraser clansmen. The Duke of Cumberland himself found my father, still alive.

"Shoot the rebel dog," he ordered. But his lieutenant refused.

"I'll give up my commission before I'll do that to Charles Fraser of Inverallochie."

So the next in line took his gun, and fired.

> *Pause.*

I swallowed those words like a fist of hot coals. The rage — to keep the rage down — a struggle — till the day I die...

> *Pause.*

When it was over, my mother dead and buried, I sold our stinking piece of bog and set out for London, to find that lieutenant and thank him...James Wolfe. Yes, I know the name makes your blood run cold, but he was an honourable man. I used my money to buy a commission. Came with him to Quebec.

I am not English born, and I despise the money-grubbing Protestants as much as any Irishman. but when I put on that Redcoat, I did it to be part of something higher than a clan or a tribe, and their endless grudges against each other.

And when I took it off, I did so to put myself at the service of something even higher. And that is the truth in any language.

***

Published by NuAge Editions.

Abandon Hope Mabel Dorothy

Wayne MacPhail

A journalist returns to the home of his natural parents in Newfoundland, 35 years after they both died and he was adopted outside the family. Originally there to research the sinking of his father's ship, he ends up researching the story of his life.

ALAN

When I was twenty I was in second year university. My parents had moved down south. I was by myself in this little rathole of an apartment. Things were going okay, but then I could see it coming in the distance, this, hopelessness. It covered me, like a shadow. I stopped caring about the world, about my friends, myself, like whatever light I had was being eaten. In the end I just lay in bed, watching ants crawl along the baseboards. One morning I found enough energy to call a cab and checked myself in. I was there for three weeks. I lost control. couldn't sleep, smoked, did group, spoke to men who smelt of chemicals, explored the lines on my hands.

Huh, I found out I had a front row seat on the edge of the abyss. There were people standing in hallways like houseplants. Men and women moving through nightmares I'd never even dreamt of, like their heads had been turned inside out. All those blind fish, mad a mummers. the doctors were pretty interested in it all. I told them the scraps I knew then about how our mother and father died. They all strapped on their hipwaders and took turns churning up the Freudian cesspool.

They said I had a profound sense of isolation I had to deal with. I wasn't in any mood to argue with them at the time. I don't think they were all that helpful, but it seemed to make them feel better. I could feel the drugs trying to pull me out from under the shadow, and I let them. The depression took care of itself, or, at least, it felt that way. It just passed overhead and I got on with my life. Like a cracked plate.

A cracked plate, that's the way one of the doctors described it. he said after a nervous breakdown people are like mended crockery, serviceable but not completely whole.

***

Available as a copyscript.

Love is Strange

Paul Ledoux & David Young

*Inspired by the story of Charles Keiling (Franz Jacob Colby),
the Canadian farmer who fell in love with Anne Murray, the
play explores the nature of obsessive love, the role of the
media and stardom in our society. Here, Colby tells his story
in the courtroom.*

COLBY

It's true...I love her. If she were here she could clear this whole thing up
in about three seconds flat, but she isn't. That's not her way. It never
has been. It's crazy, but who knows, maybe everybody who falls in
love is just a little bit crazy. See, when two people are in love they're
in each other's heads all day long, no matter what kind of distance is
between them! Love arcs like electricity...across a city...across a
country...like a halo around the world.

Now, here's what I don't understand...For nearly 10 years I wrote to
Linda, sent her presents, saw her whenever I could. For 10 years she
welcomed, even encouraged my interest. Then one day, out of the blue,
I'm arrested and thrown into jail. I was 40 years old and had never so
much as picked up a parking ticket. Suddenly, I was trapped in a legal
revolving door. I reach out towards Linda and I'm arrested. The same
charge. The same arresting officer. Even the same prosecutor — Mr.
C.G. Broilman, a classic publicity-grubbing Toronto fool. And he calls
his buddy Dr. Rand, an ambulance-chasing psychiatrist who specializes
in spewing narrow-minded notions about Linda and I for public
consumption. Of course, the press loves it.

And the result of this circus? I end up in Canada's most famous prison
for the criminally insane — Willowood Mental Health Centre,
Maximum Security Unit. For doing what? For writing a girl a love
letter.

Eight a.m. and still next to pitch black, the way it is in the middle of February, in the middle of Alberta. It had snowed a lot during the night and I'm out plowing the road up to the house ... it's funny, I can still remember the smell of Aqua Velva, a little present I bought for myself in town... and with that aroma the exact thought I have as I reach up to turn on the radio...I'm thinking about my place in the world. Thirty-three years old and what am I? A single man...on an 80-acre family farm...alone. A plane roars overhead. I look up into the darkness, and strangely, it's as if I'm up there on that plane. I look out and see myself, a tiny detail in an aerial photograph, a little blob of light on a lonely road. A man in a glass box with waves of snow up all around.

This is how it's going to be for me. Trapped in a pattern that's entirely governed by the tilt of the earth on it's axis. Six months of light and warmth where you struggle to bring in a decent crop.

Then she tilts back the other way...it gets darker and colder...until everything dies except for what's inside the little circle you draw around yourself. And then you vanish...become part of that big silence.

See...sitting there, listening to you, it was like I was stepping away from myself. I wasn't much different from a lot of guys I knew. My Dad had passed on. Mom was in a nursing home in Red Deer, and my brother, well he never much cared for farming. So there I was; "stuck with the farm." But I never saw it that way. No, I wanted that farm. I plunged right into it, tried to create my own little 800-acre universe. What I couldn't afford to buy, I'd build. What I couldn't find, I'd invent. I put up a new barn, and a windmill. I ran a model operation...but...it didn't matter. I still felt like nothing. Jacob Colby, going through the motions of working a deserted family farm.

Then that dawn, listening to you...it was like something opened in my heart and let in a burst of pure colour. Suddenly that old song I'd heard a million times seemed to make sense out of life, and the feelings I was trying to control. Both of us were caught in the same cycle of death and rebirth...in a world where love had been lost. But...a little bird was struggling against the winter wind, flying away to...the land of gentle breezes where the peaceful waters flow. A land of love.

But...what did I know about love? A dozen dates with women who didn't understand half of the things I said to them. But there you were. The radio. A voice...the simple, clear voice of a country girl who took my feelings and turned them into poetry. I think I fell for you that very moment and I didn't want to be alone any more.

***

Published in "The CTR Anthology" - University of Toronto Press.

Colours in the Storm

Jim Betts

A play with songs about the life and mysterious death of famous Canadian painter, Tom Thomson. This monologue is delivered by Larry Dixon, an Algonquin Park guide, poacher and moon-shiner. It is based on a painting of Thomson's that featured Larry chopping firewood.

> *LARRY DIXON, wearing a battered fedora and holding an axe, stands stiffly outside his shack. He speaks to the audience.*

DIXON

This here behind me's my shack. You probably recognize it. 'Course, you prob'ly recognize me for that matter...The hat — the axe?

> *He bends over in the pose of the painting, "Larry Dixon Splitting Wood".*

"Larry Dixon Splitting Wood", right? I knew you'd recognize me eventually. Hell, if I hadn't been in a private collection all them years I guess I'd be as famous as them jack pines he kept doin'. Folks say — artsy folks, anyway — that Tom wasn't all that good at paintin' people. That could be — don't really have an opinion on that. Don't know much about art, just know I like to be painted. Built this shack myself. Wasn't much. Wasn't ever meant to be. Annie Fraser come by one night — not for what you think, though some did — told me it had...what did she say?..."potential". Hell. What it had was more drafts than conscription and the plumbing quarter mile up the path. But this one spring, Tom brought this fella Lismer. And one day, when I guess this Lismer was tired o' trampin' through the woods fightin' squiters, he sat down and done this picture o' my shack. He actually took time and painted a picture o' my shack. Hell, I laughed for a week. Couldn't poach for laughin' gave me away! Some joke!

Then a couple o' months later I heard he'd sold the damn thing for $400.00 — $400.00 for a picture o' my shack. Well, I didn't know whether to laugh or cry. Some jack-ass city-slicker pays $400. to put a paintin' o' Larry Dixon's shack — oh, sorry, "The Guide's Home" — on their wall. Hell, I woulda sold 'em the whole damn shack for less than that.

Never did make much sense to me. Just goes to show ya, I guess, ya never know what's got "potential."

> *He leans over again as in "Larry Dixon Splitting Wood," holds the pose a moment then holds his hand out, grinning.*

"Larry Dixon Splitting Wood." $400.00 please.

***

Available as a copyscript.

Egats Rood

Carol Sinclair

*Martins, an actor on the outs, preens at his dressing table,
sipping scotch from a half-empty bottle.*

MARTINS

It's been an exhausting opening. Prefaced by an unusually arduous
rehearsal process. Oh, not particularly so for me. No. Never for me.
You see, I never get the plum roles, the beef steaks.

No. I mostly sit fetally in a corner, chin on hands, hands on knees and
watching the work of others. From Chekov, Ibsen and Wilde through
Ayckbourn, Shakespeare and Shaw, I'm as well-read as any, more's the
pity, for I've never in my life been tossed a juicy one.

Always too thin, too tall, too strident, too weak to play the meaty
leads. Always too something, and never, it seems, enough of
anything...

But the state of exhaustion favours no man. Throughout my alleged
career, I've commonly found my three quarters of an hour's daily
contribution as wearing as those who've actually gotten up and worked.

It's the waiting, you see. The hope against false hope that yes, yes,
before dinner, the pompous pontificator known as the Director will
have been bullied sufficiently by that bull terrier called Stage
Management into reaching the scene he's promised to reach by twelve
glorious bells. It never happens.

It is no longer indecently premature of me to begin my toilet. Don my
spirit gum and yet another bad beard to obscure yet another finely
rendered performance. Something to do while I WAIT for that nematode
to return with my medical bag. Was there ever an actor so cursed with
so many broken props?

And so you move into Tech Week, where the demands of WAITING grow tenfold. Stand like a stork in wait for your lights. Freeze like a Phoenix for the lost-and-never-to-be-found sound cue. Exit. Re-enter. Exit. Re-enter. Only to be told:

"We're going back."

WAIT, while some berk with a bobbing Robertson repairs the door you were to have entered before it fell rattling to your feet. On your feet, as often as not...

WAIT, while some witch with an overt loathing for your body pins you inescapably into an ill-fitting piece of parody that will only serve to provoke critics who would otherwise not have noticed you at all.

WAIT in the morning for the tardy little tart at the box to let you bloody in.

Wait while the kettle boils, only to find they've run out of bags. And you without your Bovril.

WAIT for the last train home to whisk your weary bones away into the night.

WAIT in the queue for your dole to come in. WAIT for your agent to bloody call, oblivious to the knowledge that your phone's been disconnected while you WAITED for your dole to come in. WAIT for the call-back, WAIT for the outcome, WAIT for the chap to get to the line:

"It's not the lead, Old String, but a very nice bit just the same." WAIT for rehearsal to begin. WAIT for the opening, only to long...for closing.

***

Available from the author - contact Playwrights Union of Canada.

Crackpot

Rachel Wyatt

Based on the novel of the same name by Adele Wiseman. Hoda, the heroine is a "crackpot", but also a practical young woman who does what she has to do to provide her blind father, Danile, with food and warmth, in desperate times in Winnipeg between two world wars. Here her father describes his forced separation from his mother and his arranged marriage.

DANILE

I heard the sickness enter our house. I could hear it in my mother's breath, heard it wrestling with her. Heard her pleading with it. Heard its cry of triumph.

And she screamed at me: 'Don't come near me, Danile. Stay away.'

Not to come. Not to go. What was I to do? I stood at the door yelling, 'People! People! Help us!'

Then I took my Book and sang all the holy words I knew. And so the people came. But not to save her. No.

It was a hot clammy day when they carried me from the house. I struggled like a wild thing, slithering about in their hands and my sweat.

They tried to explain to me what they were going to do but all I knew was it was wrong to leave my sick mother. So there I was, a blind boy, being led to meet his bride in the city of the dead.

When all else fails, Hodaleh, there is an action which can be taken. A gesture which, made properly and with God's blessing, can restore the forces of life where only the forces of death had reigned before.

***

Published by Playwrights Canada Press.

Body and Soul

John Mighton

To what extent is our desire conditioned, and what forms will our desire take when we are given the means to simulate any experience? The author takes us to a place where love, biology, and technology meet.

SCIENTIST

Let's face it — sex is no longer primarily for reproduction. So there's no need to have a real body there. One day we'll be able to transmit sensations directly to the brain — you'll see bodies moving and responding, feel textures and pressures, whatever the computer conjures up. And the pleasure people will feel will far surpass anything they feel in sex. It'll change the way they relate to each other. People will form bonds based on friendship rather than sex. Real physical beauty will no longer be important. Because no one can be as beautiful as an image. Until now the world was the only reality. And it was hard to change. In virtual reality people will be able to change things as they please. In the real world there are shortages, but not in the world of images. It will be the beginning of real social change. Democracy isn't simply a condition of free political choice. A society where everyone can vote but where the vast majority are continually denied the fulfillment of their desires isn't a democracy. People won't be free until everyone can have and do exactly the same things.

***

Published by Coach House Press.

River Lady

David Widdicombe

A female drifter meets a disgruntled dishwasher in an all-night diner. She collects marbles from every town she visits and longs for a life as comforting as K-Mart. He wants to start a religion inspired by the movie "Planet of the Apes".

TYLER

I never had religion in my life before. Maybe 'cause I never really understood it. The way I saw it if you wanted ta be religious you had ta be always buying stuff. Like steak knives or glow-in-the-dark statues of Jesus. I saw this one guy on TV that said he would have an epileptic fit, live, coast to coast if people didn't buy his entire stock of Mary Magdalene pocket flashlights. You shoulda seen those phones start ringing. I just figured religion was an excuse to sell things you couldn't sell in normal department stores. Then somethin' happened that changed my life. This guy stopped me on the street and asked me if I was a Christian. And I thought about it a minute and I figured I was so I said sure I'm a Christian and he said I couldn't be a Christian unless I'd been saved and I told him I was pulled outta the ice once and he said that didn't count. So I broke his nose. And then I knocked out two of his teeth. And I got ta thinkin' what's the point of belonging to a religion where ya always haveta live up ta someone else's standards and follow someone else's rules? So you know what I'm gonna do? I'm gonna create my own religion. I'm gonna base it on the movie "Planet of the Apes." Don't laugh. There's a lotta philosophy in that movie. And philosophy is the basis of any religion. I remember the first time I saw "Planet of the Apes." It was in the diner where I wash dishes. In the kitchen we got this little black and white monochrome sittin' up on the top shelf next to the condiments and one night I come in for my shift and it's already on and the short-order cook's starin' up at it like he's hypnotized or somethin'. So I look up at the TV and I see all these talkin' apes ridin' horses and shootin' rifles and treatin' Charlton Heston worse than the Romans ever did — and I think it must be a comedy so I start laughin' my head off. And Cookie turns ta me and he says, "Shut up man. This is serious shit." So I start watchin' it more closely. Pretty soon I can't take my eyes off it. I get involved. And you know that part at the end when Chuck's ridin' along the beach with his girlfriend and all of a sudden he comes face to face with the Statue of Liberty stickin' outta the sand? It was such a shock I nearly pissed myself. Little did I know that was the closest I'd ever get ta havin' a religious experience. I wish I thought about startin' the religion then. But the revelation I had some time later was that when Chuck starts poundin' his fist in the sand and yellin' up at what's left of Lady Liberty 'cause he knows he's really on Earth and that they blew it up — he's not just rantin' at the statue — he's rantin' at stupidity. He's rantin' at everythin' mankind ever screwed up. He's damnin' war and pollution and poverty and greed and racism and plastic diapers and terrorists — he's damnin' politicians and soldiers and criminals — he's damnin' us. Human beings. If you stop and think about it, it's pretty disgusting bein' a human being, isn't it? That's why I wanta be an ape. You don't see apes droppin' cigarette butts and candybar wrappers all over the place. You don't see apes wandering inta schoolyards with an Ouzi. 'Course I don't actually mean we turn into apes. I mean we just return to the basics. Eating and sleeping and fucking. Surviving. Things couldn't be any worse than they are now. Not in a million years.

***

Available as a copyscript.

Fairy Blood

Peter Eliot Weiss

The story of a neurotic coming out of the closet. He believes he is being interrogated by a cardboard cut-out policeman, and begins to confess all his secrets.

MR. DID-YOU-WASH-YOUR-HANDS

There I was on the seawall last summer. Trying. Taking a walk, you know, around dinner time. And I passed a guy I'd seen the night before at a club. He was a fantasy of a guy except he was real. He was young and good-looking and, of course, muscular. The way a lot of the guys are nowadays at the clubs. Like, as if they go to the gym every day and do an extra special long workout just before they go dancing to pook out their pecs just a little bit more. Well, this guy had obviously been pooking his pecs that very afternoon, because he was looking very pooky sitting there beside this huge gym bag, twisting and torquing his torso trying to work out the knots in the shoulder blade area. And I thought, oh I bet you he's just waiting for someone to come along and say something like, "Hey, looks like you could use some practiced hands on that taut and tired trapesius of yours." Someone...

Me! Could I do that? Was this my chance? My big chance? Was the closet door swinging open at last. "Hey, looo....looo..." Wait a second. What if I was wrong? What if he wasn't waiting for some stranger to come along and talk to him, take him away, give him a massage, make love to him. What if he already had a date and he was just waiting innocently 'cause this was where they had decided to meet? What if I walked over to him and started talking and this guy came over, six foot eight, 270 pounds and said, "Hey, what do you think you're doing talking to my boyfriend? I'm going to kill you now." It's possible. It is possible. So I decided better safe than sorry and I kept on walking. But twenty minutes later, when I came back, he was still there. Sitting in the same spot, massaging the same shoulder. No date. No boyfriend. No danger. And it hit me again. He's just waiting for someone to walk by and notice him, someone who's kind and gentle and understanding.

Someone he could talk to as he took off his shirt, someone to pour almond-scented oil on his smooth skin, knead his knotted muscles...
I was just about to say something when this other guy came up. A real beauty, young and tough, dangerous looking. The kind of guy who still wears tight T-shirts with cigarette packs rolled in the sleeve and gets away with it. He was walking his dog. You know, in dreams dogs represent male sexuality. This was a big dog, handsome, a kind of Doberman or something.

And it hits me. This guy, this tough guy, he's out looking for somebody to pick up. Somebody to say, "Nice dog. Nice BIG dog! I sure would like to pet that big dog of yours." But he walks right past me and right past the boy on the bench. Without so much as looking at either of us. So maybe I'm wrong. Maybe he's just walking his dog. He takes a 90-degree turn and goes out to the end of the beach, to the end of this rocky spit that protrudes way out into the water and he gets down on his knees on the rocks and he hugs the dog. Kisses it. Rubs the fur, real rough, real affectionate. You know, just a beautiful, unbridled exhibition of man/dog love. Very ostentatious. Then he gets up, comes back toward us, me and the bench boy, then stops and waits for a moment, in silence. Looking out to sea. A portrait of a man, his dog and his aspiration. Is that the right word? Aspiration? Don't know. Then he passes me, passes the bench and leaves the seawall. A slight pause.

(*slight pause*) The bench boy gets up, picks up his huge gym bag and follows the tough boy. Next they appear together, walking side by side, with the dog between them, cresting the hill. You see? I was right! I was right! The boy on the bench had been waiting to get picked up. The other one was looking for someone.

Oh! and the way it happened! Wasn't that magnificent! In silence. Just like that. Like a dream or a movie or a cliché. Absolutely perfect. I knew it! And I knew what was happening back at the apartment right now. As clear as if it was happening to me. Footsteps in the shadowy hallway. The clinging smell of suppers cooking behind other doors. Muffled TV sounds. Key in the lock. Heart beating faster. Door swinging open. Then shut. Slam! Bam! Grab! Clutch! Arms! Legs! Butts! Groins! Tongues! Throats! Hands! Clothes! Flesh! Hands! Hands? Wait a second. He had dog hands.

I mean, after all that stuff with the dog. You get in the door, you know. Did he go, first thing and wash? No. I mean, dog hands, they smell, and how do you ask, in the heat of the moment? It would certainly break the spell, to say, in the touching and the clutching and the grabbing and the licking, um, excuse me, I'm really sorry, but you know, I hate to mention this, but your hands with your dog...do you think...I mean, I hope you wouldn't mind very much...

I'm allergic to dogs, you see. I get all stuffed up and a rash on my neck that's really, really itchy and my eyes get itchy and red and then I start to get asthmatic and breathe like (*he demonstrates asthmatic breathing*). I would have had to take a pill. I usually have one on me...but, you know, even with the pill...dog hands. (*pause*)

So, there I was on the beach, with the image of the boys fading as the last of the light drained out of the sky into the bay. (*pause*)

When I told my friends what happened, they laughed. They started calling me Mr. Did-You-Wash-Your-Hands. They say, "Well, has Mr. Did-You-Wash-Your-Hands been going to the clubs lately? Is Mr. Did-You-Wash-Your-Hands planning to pick somebody up one night?"

***

Available as a copyscript.

All the Verdis of Venice

Normand Chaurette
Translated by Linda Gaboriau.

*Taken hostage, Italian composer Giuseppe Verdi is compelled
at gunpoint to write a patriotic opera within 48 hours. In this
play Chaurette delves into the relationship between art,
politics and nationalism. The play is about the megalomaniac,
tragic, and passionate world of the opera.*

THE PROMPTER

Why? I'm used to it. Besides, I'm the last one who'd be surprised to see
them appear to the tune of words I am the first to say, words I've been
saying for ages. I often feel as if I am summoning ghosts. "Casta
diva"... Imagine! The curtain has just risen, and the minute they appear,
those poor cantatrices who can barely control their stage fright have to
sing either a B flat or a straight B or a high C... "Casta Diva..." I've
seen Bellini taking stock more often than I've seen "Norma" succeed.
The composer appears in the shadows, looking distressed, since he feels
contrite about terrifying men and women for centuries to come, simply
because he couldn't resist the temptation of applying ink to a space just
a touch above the scale, without even straining his fingers. Now he
must pay for the power he possessed in his lifetime. The power to
make souls swoon in a single, dizzying instant, but also the power to
snap the vocal cords of the greatest in the world of opera, Mercadante,
Colonnese, Benza, poor Teresa Stok! All would rather die forgotten
than find themselves on stage stranded in their own silence. That's why
the composer reappears to offer a word of consolation, first to them,
then to himself. Sometimes the distraught eyes of this strange couple
come to rest on the floor whose boards sustain my own gaze, and I have
seen vast deserts swept by more remorse contained in art than art
contains ambition. Remorse is sand and triumph an oasis. The tear-
filled eyes of the composer and his singer seek in mine the mirror of
their grief, a glimmer of comprehension, a vague sense of
compassion...but I am only the prompter. I can offer no tears to reflect
theirs. My eyes are as dry as an insomniac's, because they remain

riveted to the tiny lines of the libretto! What if I were to fail in my duty! Here I am, a humble hunchback and shortsighted at that, so nothing I have witnessed has taken place beyond the tip of my nose. I have seen Isolde die beneath my gaze, but I've seen nothing of her love for Tristan, nor of the sea and sky. I have seen Don Juan perish countless times, but I've never been able to admire the extravagance of his feast. Bah, what's the point? Who cares about my complaints? I am an ignorant prompter in charge of the words but not the tone. My task is simply to deliver the words to others, knowing that someone else will promptly say them better. I accepted long ago to whisper in the dark words I would have preferred to save for myself, instead of listening to their echo reverberate for the multitude. Oh, woe unto him who claims that a libretto is a mediocre thing, for that is where I have drawn the very stuff of my knowledge. I would have gladly remained ignorant of passion; I'd be the first to say that love is a sham. There is no work more thankless than mine. There's no sense in dreaming of promotions — what future is there for a prompter? Where can someone go who has spent his life in a hole? Whispering words would be frowned upon under any other circumstances, and aside from those who try to cure the mad, who would be interested in me? The conductor? He ignores me. I am the only one he can't see. The opera directors? They come and go without ever realizing that great things have small beginnings. Very small. *Pianissimo.* Then, from *pianissimo* to *piano*, and from *piano* to *mezzo forte*, and from *forte* to *più forte*, and then *fortissimo...si, comè un colpo di canòne.* You know, given all the contrived anguish and all the deaths that take place here before my very eyes, and since it is true, for you as well as for me, that everything is feasible and all manner of apparition possible, to answer your question, Rinuccio Terziani, no, oh no, the resurrection of those who imagined all this is not about to terrify me.

***

Available from centre des auteurs dramatiques - Montréal.

Canada's Golgotha

Mark Leiren Young

A play inspired by a true story about a sculpture by Derwent Wood that was considered so dangerous it was removed from an exhibit of Canadian art depicting World War I, and hidden away until the 1990s. Wood is in his forties.

WOOD

I signed up. Offered my services to the cause. And the sergeant who took my name asked what I could do, what unique skills I had to contribute. And he looked at me like I was nothing, because I was too old to fight and too feeble to dig ditches. I told him that I had no military skills but I would do what I could. I would serve my country. And he asked my occupation. And I said proudly, I am a sculptor. And he laughed, like I'd said I was a clown, or a fire-eater, or a member of Parliament. And then he stopped laughing and I could tell he was appraising me to see what I was made of, and I knew at that moment that I had made a dreadful mistake. He asked if I would, indeed, do anything, and stout with patriotism I declared that of course I would. And then he scrawled a name and address on a slip of paper. It was a hospital, a special hospital. For soldiers who had been discharged with...injuries. Severe injuries.

They called them...

Men who had lost their limbs, their eyes, parts of their face...and when the doctors and the nurses at this special hospital found out who I was, what I did, they looked at me like I could help them. One of the doctors knew of my work, thought that surely a man with my skill would be able to reconstruct what these men had lost. Reconstruct their flesh with metal. It was all I could do to bring myself to look at them. To force a smile and a few words of encouragement as I measured what remained of them for my prosthetics.

I've spent my life striving to create beauty and here I was, using all the skill at my command, every trick I'd ever learned. everything I knew, to create monsters. Monsters with metal jaws, plates where their cheeks used to be, creatures from my worst nightmares. And the more lifelike the prosthetic I created, the more hideous they appeared to me. As if I was mocking God.

One private, a Scot, had been...a bomb from his own unit, it went off by mistake. That was the only reason he survived, because, since he was on their side of the line they were able to send him back right away before the fighting started. He couldn't talk, of course. I don't know how he could breathe. But he could. I sat with him, talked, barber shop chatter. I said I would do what I could. I measured and I fitted, but I don't think I ever really looked.

And I went back to my studio and I worked on crafting his...face. And I swear on my life that never, never have I worked on anything with more care and more diligence. No drop of whisky while I was making this. No sleep either. No real sleep. I kept thinking of this boy. And when I finished it, I felt like Michelangelo must have when he completed his David. And the doctors, and the nurses, when they saw what I'd done, they cooed over me like I had just discovered penicillin or a cure for cancer.

The next day I came to see him, my young Scot, with the face that I had built him. And there he was, eyes shut, resting in his bed. And I looked at him, really looked at him. And I threw up. And God forgive me, because he wasn't asleep, and he saw me, he saw my horror and my shame and if I'd had a knife at that moment I would have slit my throat before I had time to draw another breath.

And this man with no face put his arm out to console me...and I pulled away.

***

Available from author - contact Playwrights Union of Canada.

An Investigation Into the Strange Case of the Wildboy

Sky Gilbert

Dr. Paul Verkracht, a psychologist, falls in love with the Wildboy.

VERKRACHT

I have this, a...problem. If you can call it that. No. I think you can call it a problem — why not call it a problem? If I was a tragic hero it would be a fatal flaw. But I'm not a tragic hero, no that's silly, God no...just so you'll know I can't believe I'm telling you this — well I'm a little drunk. I never get drunk, no. I know people say that but I actually never get drunk...Canadian wine, that's the problem, they say it's as good as French but it's not, you can tell, anyway, I'm a little drunk and I'm grabbing a hold of you at this function and pestering you, imposing myself on you, you're embarrassed. I should stop but, I think you should know, I have to tell somebody, what my problem is...my problem is...I believe in love.

(*pause*) Don't you think that's a problem? You don't? I think it is...no I don't mean love of a dog or love of parents. I mean...romantic love — you know — kissy kissy, the whole thing. The whole banana. The big wazoo, the movies, you know. I believe in that. I believe it's possible. But of course I also believe that romantic love contains everything within it which makes it impossible. It is a kind of dialectical model — jealousy, passion, uncertainty, insecurity, fantasy, selfishness, self*less*ness. It's all impossible but absolutely necessary and it self-destructs and yet somehow I believe that it will not. And I believe that all human beings need it even though it self-destructs and they believe it must last forever even though it doesn't. It's kind of like God.

(*pause*) And just like God, if love didn't exist human beings would have to invent it. I believe in "love". That's my tragic flaw. If I were a hero. But I'm not...I'm just a...guy. Just an ordinary guy. An ordinary...

bumbling guy. Not too attractive...attractive enough. I don't know. This is stupid, I'm drunk, and I'm embarrassing you, and I'm stepping out of character somewhat, not completely, somewhat. See that's one of my problems, I hedge. I don't go all the way. I wouldn't kill to keep... shit...this wine...I'm getting a headache. I'm sorry to bother you — I've obviously bothered you. Excuse me, I have to get on with..."things." Excuse me. Excuse me. Sorry. If you see me again sometime, somewhere, someday, you don't need to speak to me. My feelings won't be hurt. Honestly.

***

Available as a copyscript.

Coyote City

Daniel David Moses

*JOHNNY, a Native, is newly deceased but does not realize he
is a ghost customer at the Silver Dollar Bar.*

JOHNNY

Give me a drink. I need a drink. Shit. I'm over here you bugger. I'm
almost empty here. Come on and dispense with the booze.

Please man, I'm good for it. You can trust me. I'll pay you tomorrow
first thing. Come on. Come on, man, really.

Hey you want my knife? It's a real beaut. Look at all the things, man,
the gadgets. Hey, you can even cut your toenails. Come on, guy, just
one more beer. Shit.

Hey, how about a date with a real doll? Shit man, she's fresh from the
bush. I'll give you her number. Real pretty Indian chick. What do you
say? What do you say?

How about a story my Grandad gave me? A real good story, man. A
love story. Come on, man, the ladies really love to hear this story. Shit
it gets them all loose. You like loose ladies, don't you? Just another
beer, man, just one. That's all.

(*to the darkness*) Acting like I'm not here, like he can't see me. Acting
like I'm just another drunk Indian. Think he thinks I've had enough? Do
you think that too? Do you think I've had enough? Enough. Shit. You
think I've had too much. Well, who the fuck are you anyway? I don't
know you. I don't know you. Shit you're not even real. I know I need a
drink when I meet you. I look at you and I need a drink. Hey you're
nothing but a bunch of spooks. That's why I got the shakes. You're the
ones took Coyote in when he was looking for his woman. But no way
you're tricking me. No way. I'm too smart for you. You can't get away
with all that stuper-shitting with me. You're not going to get away

with anything with me. You're going to buy me a drink. Shit ya, you're going to buy me a fucking drink.

***

Published by Williams-Wallace Publishers Inc.

Mad Boy Chronicle

Michael O'Brien

*An earthy, vigorous and humourous tale based on the same legend
of the mad Danish prince on which Shakespeare also based his
play, "Hamlet".*

> *Morning. A remote hill overlooking the sea.
> FENGO, Viking lord of Helsingor, tries to lure the
> mad boy to drop his dreams of treason, and join him
> in his conquest of the north. Some spelling is
> phonetic to stress dialect.*

FENGO

Look Madd Boy. Look out at the Sea.
Don't it bestirr yer blood? It stirrs mine.
Come closer ladd. Look back at the valley.
See; what a beautiful land we live in.

You know ladd, the poets, the ancient saga-writers,
They tell us Love's the mightiest thing on earth.
Dost believe that sonn? Ist Love? Or is it Hate?
Can Love move a Mountain? Can Love win a War?
Can it, sonn? Hate can.

Witness us, us the Viking people:
Were't Love what made us rulers o' the world?
Were't Love what stood us up 'gainst Mother Natures' blast?
Ohhhh Nature, from Time's Dawn she despised us,
We, her battered children, hated her right back.
See! how we battle her, since time immemorial,
But we're winning, boy; we're winning—
Praise our swords, we rise!

Madd Boy, hear us it's time t'quit yer shammin'.
You int no Christian, nor no Fool;

All o' this Love talk, bout Jesus, bout Mary,
It's a plot to keep us Strongmen down!
And that int natural sonn. It's perverse.
Skews the Fatal Majestie of Heaven.
Fengo won't have it.

Men of Greatness should brace themselves together,
'Gainst the risin' tide of mediocre muck.
Fear it sonn, fear it, a world ruled by weaklings.
We gots to stick together, and stand tall.
Love sputts and flickers, a faint and fleeting firefly
Hate will one day engulf the sunn;
Let not our Hates drive our hearts asunder,
But bond us, boy, bond us—
Meld our hearts with shining gold!
Aye sonn — Gold!
Gold and power, sonn, my second in command. Clever Madd Boy!
Thour't proved a cunning foe.
Try using those skills for something grander.

***

Available as a copyscript.

Medea's Disgust

John Lazarus

*A bizarre public lecture by Professor Lorne Pender, a critic,
failed novelist and convicted criminal, on a best-selling novel
by his former protégé, with whom he is still obsessively in
love.*

PENDER

The next time I saw her, it was in the last place I would have expected
to find a teen-age college kid: at a University faculty party. I was at this
event because I was seeking a position in the Department of Literature.
Mein host was the Dean of Creative Writing, Professor Sidney
Feinstein.

Sidney and I go 'way back. We had been students together: the rival
shining lights, the brave young hope of our class. A friendly rivalry,
mind you. Except where it came to women. His ploy with women was
to play the Socialistic, Sympathetic, Understanding, Good Listener —
the type who used his sensitivity like a blunt instrument.

Anyway, the night of the party, there was Ondine, looking rather
adolescent and affected with the Rat on her shoulder. And then Sidney
came over, squatted beside her, protective arm around her, "Lorne, have
you met my date, Ma'amselle St. Foi?" I got quite depressed.

But then, later that evening, we played a party game called 'Erudition or
Contrition." The Eruditions are obscure academic trivia questions. If
you can't answer the question, you perform the Act of Contrition: you
expose your buttocks to the rest of the company for ten seconds of
applause. Ladies had the option of baring their breasts. Professorial sort
of game.

That evening I saw us all through Ondine's eyes: a bunch of noisy
drunken self-important middle-aged bores, mooning and flashing our

sagging body part hysterically. And then came her turn to pick an Erudition out of the hat.

It was to sing a song in a dead language, from memory, no hymns or Christmas carols permitted. She asked for a moment to think. For the first time, the room fell silent. Poor kid, we were going to have to see her breasts. Sidney began to demonstrate his anti-sexist sensitivity with a little speech suggesting that those who didn't want to play had the option of—

But then Ondine began to sing.

Singing.

Omnia sol temperat, purus et subtilis,
Novo mundo reserat faciem Aprilis.
Ad amorem properat animus herilis,
Et iocundis imperat deus puerilis

And two more verses, sung with a radiance to which I cannot do justice. Even the Rat was quiet. And when she finished, one of the professors said, "I heard the word 'deus' in there, that makes it a hymn, show us your tits, darling." I told him it was from *Carmina Burana*, and this clown said, "Oh, I know that, Lorne darling, and the *Carmina* were pagans hymns.

And then the whole crowd began to argue about whether there was such a thing as a pagan hymn — and Ondine looked me straight in the eye and said, almost inaudibly in the hubbub, "It's a love song". And I shouted, "May I have the honour of performing the Act of Contrition on the lady's behalf?' Again, the room fell silent. And I began to undo my trousers.

She almost let me get my pants down. But then she sighed a little sigh, and this teen-age college student, in a room full of university profs, said — I quote — "No, Dr. Pender, that's all right, everyone here is familiar with the art of compromise."

And with her right hand she held her sweater down while with her left hand she yanked it up, exposing one perfect caramel left breast. And she looked around the room with her head held high and the Rat perched on her shoulder. And everyone looked at the floor in shame. Except me. She and I looked at each other, and she smiled and said, "But thank you for your gallant offer to lower your trousers. Perhaps another time."

***

Available as a copyscript.

Jessica

Linda Griffiths in collaboration with Maria Campbell.

A half-breed woman embarks on a spiritual journey. SAM is JESSICA's lover. They have had a physical fight and he has used his strength to beat her.

SAM

(*reaching for JESSICA*) Baby, you okay? (*as she pushes him away*) I'm sorry babe. I'm so sorry I can't afford to be gentle, all I know is that when I see red, I fight. It's too dangerous any other way. You can't ask me why. I fight. That's what I do. Somehow that's what I'm supposed to do but it gets all screwed up. There's a place for it, I know there is, but I don't know where. You look at me, all bruised up, and you think you're the one that's hurt, but it's me that's dying. I want to beat you because I can't beat them, you're just one step down from me, that's all. You're the one thing around that's lower than me. You've gotta support me, you've gotta believe in me, even when I'm an asshole...somewhere in this world I've got to be right. They did take our balls away, and they hold them dangling in front of us while we rage around and try to get them back. All we've got is rage. I can feel myself switching when I'm strong, feel myself losing the bear, he just walks away on me. You've got your mysteries, all I've got is that sometime I was a warrior. So I'll get drunk and sing and pound the drum, dance in the gutter. There's got to be somebody out there dancing. That's all that's left of war.

***

Published by Coach House Press in "The Book of Jessica".

Steps

Janet Feindel

An exploration of personal growth from a number of perspectives. The characters emerge from various walks of life. Joe is a man who has been on the fast track and is struggling to understand who he is. He's trying to face facts and smell the 'burnt coffee.'

JOE

Look, I was shooting up rubbing alcohol. I wanted to die when I came in here. Some of youse were still buying groceries, not me. Now, I can actually rent a video, buy some chips, go home. I could never do that. Some of you are driving down a country lane. Me, I'm on the 401, if I slip here, I die. You can afford to take it easier, I can't.

Be polite. We took enough shit before we got in here, we don't have to treat each other like shit now. 'Say please, say thank you.' Connie, my first sponsor, she used to say that. God, was she ugly. I was in treatment, she comes in. This short little woman, smoking a cigar, wearing these strange pants, looking so fucking happy all the time. Jesus I hated her. She'd smile and ask me how I was doing. Shit, she pissed me off. Anyhow, after treatment she took me to my first meeting. I hated her. I was embarrassed by her, because she was so ugly. I mean ugly. I told her, 'I've got to find a sponsor.'

She said, 'I'm your sponsor.' Nowadays we are too shy about saying things like that. We're afraid to stand by our recovery.

So Connie was my sponsor. But I was embarrassed, because she was a woman and I was this big macho guy. So I said, 'Okay, temporary sponsor.' She sponsored me for seven years. Then she got cancer. Her cancer is in remission now. She volunteers in a hospice and she helps so many people. And you know, today, I figure, it was God's sense of humour that she was ugly 'cause if she hadn't been ugly, I would have hit on her. When I first met her — I was ashamed of her at meetings —

'cause of her ugliness and the cigar. Now I love Connie. And I am so proud she was my sponsor. And I'm proud to have her as a friend.

***

Available from the author - contact Playwrights Union of Canada.

Fables for the Modern World

Diana Kolpak

Cliff, a man anywhere from 28 to 45 years old who works for a large company in a large city. He considers himself something of a social misfit and has a secret plan to save the world.

CLIFF

My mother died several years ago, after selling the family house to move to Florida with the dream of becoming the developer of high-tech condominiums for retired Canadians. When she called me to announce her plan I was skeptical but wished her well. Unfortunately, the Greyhound bus in which she was making her southward migration spontaneously combusted while at a rest stop in one of the Carolinas. Mother was inside its bathroom at the time. She never risked using the rest room while the bus was moving, she said it was too dangerous. The authorities could not explain this freak accident. I suspected that it may have had something to do with mother's penchant for sneaking cigarettes and gin in the bathroom, but this theory has never been confirmed.

All of the cash from the sale of the modest family estate — a post-war bungalow — had been in my mother's clutch purse at the time of the combustion. She didn't trust banks. The accident was officially ruled an 'Act of God' by the insurance company, so there were no life insurance benefits forthcoming to any of the families of the twenty-seven victims. That was fine. I haven't been financially dependent on my mother for many years.

I do my job and do a good job. Take pride in the simple order I impose on stacks of figures and sheaves of paper. Order from chaos: my contribution to the world. Who knows what would happen if I fell down from my duty? I have become so proficient at my task that it takes only half a mind to achieve it. Half a mind. So, I have room to pursue my dreams as I sort and stamp, stamp and shuffle my way to a worry-free retirement at fifty-five. What more could one ask for?

The one pastime I have been turning to more and more of late is a study of underwater ecosystems. My interest could even be termed a passion. I often catch myself staring at nothing, imagining life deep under the sea. Water has displaced the air, but there is no need for artificial breathing devices. The air has simply become...thick, lending everything a grace, a beauty not possible in a life above the water's embrace.

Sometimes I imagine myself as part of a coral reef: solid, stately, completely fundamental to the balance of the ecosystem. More often, though, I picture myself as one of the industrious bottom feeders, although occasional flights of fancy turn me into a manta ray, but more because they can cover themselves completely in sand than for their exotic appearance.

The dangers and rules seem much more clear-cut in the sea. Eat or be eaten. Coexist with your neighbours. Evolve. Reproduce. Die. So simple.

***

Available from the author - contact Playwrights Union of Canada.

All Fall Down

Wendy Lill

CONNORS is the social worker investigating a case of alleged sexual abuse in a daycare centre.

CONNORS

How do you protect yourself from the images floating around out there? How do you protect yourself from the pictures inside your own head?

A man bounces his daughter on his lap, sits on the bed, watches his wife undress, thinks about winter tires, the teller with the big hooters at the bank, how he'd like to reach out and stroke them, his coldsore, his daughter's musical giggles, the bruise on his wife's leg, how soft the little girl's cheeks are, how sweet she smells. He may even wonder about if she was fifteen years older and not his daughter, but that's gone in an instant and he's remembering his own mother's scent, her shining hair, sitting on her lap, feeling like the only special one in the world...and suddenly, he despises his wife, wants to strangle her, but just for an instant. For an instant he wants to end his own life too, all the gaping nights, weeks, years ahead, all those dark unexplored holes behind, and then that's gone too. Thoughts fly by like hummingbirds. Some of them could land you in jail but you keep them in your head and they're harmless there.

I respect the mind but I'm afraid of it. There are snakes and field mice, rats and doves, lions and bunnies sleeping side by side...it's a miracle. It's a popping swirling miracle. And now they're all waking up together and it scares me to death. (*ironic*) Are we making progress here? Are we easing the pain? Start at the beginning. Did all the pieces fit? Was it seamless. It was a time in my life when I thought I had all the answers.

***

Published by Talonbooks.

Office Hours

Norm Foster

Warren Kimble is a disgruntled news reporter for a big city television station. In this scene, he is rehearsing a speech he is going to make to his boss.

WARREN

You twit. You fat-ankled, capricious, inarticulate, tofu-eating twit.

(*beat*) No, that might be too confrontational. Uh...all right, let's try this.

You know something, Miss Gerard? Mrs. Gerard? Pam? Can I call you Pam, Pam?

No, the more I say it, the more it sounds like Spam. All right. Pamela.

Pamela, I'm given to understand you don't like my work.

No, too civil. Be a little more intimidating. Give it the Robert DeNiro inflection.

Pamela, I hear you've got a problem with my work. You got a problem with my work? Are you serious? You can't be serious. *My* work? Are you tellin' me you got a problem with my work?

No, wait. Start off with a joke. Something light before I tear that strip off of her. All right. All right.

Pam, don't you think it's funny that my name is Warren *Kimble* and yours is Pam *Gerard*? Huh? Kimble, Gerard? We've got kind of a "Fugitive" thing happening here. Kind of a David Janssen, Barry Morse kind of thing...

No, forget the jokes. Get right to the point. Straight and direct.

Pam, I get the feeling that you don't like my work. Well, let me tell you something. Right now, I don't like my work either. and I'll tell you why, Pam. I'm a reporter. A *news* reporter. I've been working my way up for twenty-three years. That's right, Pam. some of us work our way up. We don't marry the station manager and go from Kinsmen bingo Hostess to news producer just like that. But that's neither here nor there, no, that doesn't bother me one goddamned bit. what bothers me is that I used to be a good newsman. Hell, I was the top reporter in this city at one time. I did stories that mattered. Stories with integrity. Stories I was proud of. And now? Two Weeks ago I covered a memorial and wake for a racehorse. What the hell is that? So the horse died. Who gives a shit? It's not Black Beauty for Godssake. And last week you sent me to interview that Pentecostal group that wanted to put a loin clothe on the statue of Cupid. so, there I am interviewing the queen of the tight-asses while cupid urinates into a fountain behind me. Boy, there was a proud moment in my journalistic career. How am I supposed to do good work in a situation like that, you unenlightened, dizzy-eyed, Melrose Place-watching, scrotum-cracking harpy. I need the hard-hitting stories. And I'm not talking about doing *Death of a Salesman* every night. Just something newsworthy. That's all I ask. I mean, I'm the senior reporter here. I deserve first crack at those stories. Oh, and there's another thing, I'm forty-eight years old, Pam. I'm old, and I feel old. Too old to have to start worrying about losing my job. I've got a mortgage I'm paying off and a kid I'm trying to put through university. That's a school, Pam. A big one with people your age in it. So that's it. That's all I have to say. And if you want to fire me, you go right ahead. You go right the hell ahead, because quite frankly, lady, I don't give a tinker's toot.

Oh, and one more thing. I don't appreciate being summoned into your office like one of your underlings and then being left here to ponder my fate while you get called away on some petty emergency. You understand what I'm saying, you canker-nosed, Cat Stevens-loving, pulp-headed malfeasance? Warren Kimble waits for no one!

***

Available from the author - contact Playwrights Union of Canada.

Lilies

Michel Marc Bouchard
Translated by Linda Gaboriau

*A romantic drama. Simon Doucet, a convict now, re-enacts for
Jean Bilodeau, now a Roman Catholic bishop, their fiery past
as lovers, while rehearsing "The Martyrdom of Saint
Sebastian". This is from the epilogue, where Bilodeau explains
his drastic actions to Simon.*

BILODEAU

Sodom! Sodom and Gomorrah! It was Sodom and Gomorrah that was
burning, and I was God, with the right to decide whether you would live
or die. May God forgive me. May He grant me His mercy for the
sacraments my hands have blessed. I couldn't understand the force that
drew you together. The force that allowed you to overcome the
beatings, a father's rejection, the public humiliation, a mother's death,
the temptation of wealth and of a better life elsewhere...A force so
strong you were willing to die. I thought I could possess that force by
running away with the two of you, but you rejected me right up to the
last second. (*pause*) I finally managed to get the attic door open.
Everything was on fire. You and Vallier were lying there in each other's
arms, dying. I went up to you. The fire was coming closer and closer. I
tore you out of Vallier's arms and dragged you away from the flames. I
went back to get Lily-White but just as I got close to him...I could hear
your "never, never" echoing louder and louder. Never, Bilodeau! Never!
Never! I turned on my heels and left him there. I closed the door behind
me. It was Sodom and Gomorrah that was burning, and I was God,
punishing you both by saving you and letting him die.

I wanted you to remember me. I wanted you to go on thinking of me, I
didn't care how or what. When I testified against you, I knew that in
prison you'd never stop thinking of me. And I succeeded. Oh, my
archers, let my destiny be fulfilled. Let me die at the hands of men. Kill
me! Kill me! I loved you so much I wanted to destroy your soul.

***

Published by Coach House Press.

Black River Miracle

Harry Thurston and Gregory M. Cook

Angus, 57, is a veteran of two world wars and 40 years of mining. In this scene he comforts his son-in-law Bobby, 21, as they both await rescue from the mine after a disaster traps them.

ANGUS

The mine gets into a man. It's like goin' into The Church. You're married to her. Most of us is lifers. (*pause*) Last time anyone got outta here was the wars. And not many got away then. Me and Lenny Hill jumped the train to Halifax. Lenny said, "War is like a book. It takes you outta your own small world." Lenny was always talkin' books. We got one o' them rooms down on the Harbour. Whew, it stunk worse than a dead mine rat. Lenny says, "Did the tide go out or did somebody die in here?" (*pause*) Lenny was cursin' the mine and dreamin' of seein' the world. He'd curse the pots, the gas, the company and the government. (*pause*) But Lenny was deep. One day we was sittin' on the level, eatin' our lunch and he says: "Right here was the green forest of Africa. Funny to think about it, ain't it? Giant fern fronds, like feathers over the Pharaoh's boat. Moss on the forest floor, soft as baby's eyelashes. Big dragon flies, (*spreading his hands*) with wings like angels; the sun darting through everything. Blue sky, like the roof of the world. These rocks were ferns and palm trees growing over us. And over there the river flowed slow and black as a big snake. (*pause*) It's a good thing she was deep. Or we'd be crawling like snakes ourselves. Like the boys over in Joggins. Above us is millions and millions of years piled up like the pages of one of them tissue paper bibles. (*pause*) Every time we'd hear a little bump, Lenny would say, "Feel that river flowin' by, just like time herself?" I'd say to Lenny, "I can see what ya mean." Though there were lots of times I didn't. (*pause*) One day he said, "Angus, buddy, I want to see where this river come from!" Anyway, it was the next day we went down to the recruitin' station and lined up. Hell, I was only fifteen. But I thought they might take me if I went into the army with Lenny. Lenny went first. They made you strip down while they weighed ya and poked and peered into ya. Well, I heard the doctor say to Lenny: "Okay, Hill, You got a seam of coal from ear to ear. Get back to Black River. I figured that was it for me too. But, when the doctor looked into my ears, he didn't say a word. I can still see the hurtin' look on Lenny's face, 'cause he couldn't go. (*pause*) I've thought about that doctor. 'Spose he couldn't see the coal in my ears. He musta figured I was black on the inside too. (*pause*) It's about as easy to git outta the mine, son, as it is for me to git outta my skin. (*pause*) "It's okay, Angus," Lenny says. "You go. I'll be with the boys here. Someone's got to fire up steel to finish the war." (*pause*) Funny thing. I went through the war, even the night only seven of us in the whole company crawled out alive.

We had a victory parade down Union Street. People was wavin' after us like we was heroes. I kept lookin' in the crowd for Lenny. (*pause*) But I come home to find him gone, buried in this black river, just a month before the war was over. (*pause*) Think about all the lives that's been lived in this coal.

***

Available from authors - contact Playwrights Union of Canada.

The Plainsman

Ken Mitchell

*The first play in a trilogy documenting the settlement of the
Great Plains. It focuses on the Metis people, their struggles
during the North West Resistance of 1885, and the pivotal role
played by Gabriel Dumont, and his relationship with his wife,
Madeleine. Here he is talking to God.*

> *GABRIEL is in the main room of a shack in
> Lewistown, Montana. It is November 18, 1885.
> GABRIEL wears more conventional clothing than his
> usual buckskins.*

GABRIEL

Hey — Old Man! You there? You don't hear from me too often. But I
guess you don't mind — with all the complaints you have to listen to!
So, I didn't get to Mass too often. But I talk — inside — from the
heart. Aaaa, you know that. Listen, I got one hell of a favour to ask.
Need more time. For Louis David. About three weeks. I'm working on
it but — I gotta tell you Old Man, it's not easy working in the States.
Policemen on every street corner! And at the border — I remember the
days when it was only you out there, Old Man — now you gotta show
a piece of paper! Every time you cross the border. The Medicine Line.

So that was a real mess, eh — after Batoche? Oh, I don't blame you for
that. No, that was just bad luck. Some carelessness. We could have
smuggled him out of there in a horse blanket. But, he insisted on
putting himself in your hands, and when you were distracted for just a
minute — the Redcoats got him!

And then three months ago, eh? I nearly sprung him out of jail! Oh, it
was hard gettin' into Regina — the town practically surrounded. They
were ready for trouble — armed patrols everywhere. I couldn't turn
around without seein' my face on the posters. "Rebel general! Thousand
dollar reward." One night, two of my men arrested at the livery stable.

So I had to get out, fast. And Madeleine awful sick here in Lewistown. But we got a new plan all set to go now! Just waiting for the message from Willow Bunch. Laroque's gonna blow out the cell, middle of the night, while Isbister and some Sioux from Qu'Appelle raise a big ruckus at the Mountie barracks. Three horses down by the creek! I'll be waiting at Moose Jaw with a relay of fresh horses, then straight for the border — before they can get their bugles out of their pockets! Surprise, eh? Better than cannons, every time.

Well, like I say — we need more time, Old Man. If you could get the Pope to demand a stay of execution. The Quebec bishops have been hollering for that for months. Laroque will be ready to go any day — and when the word comes, I'll get there.

But we need your help, Old Man. Even two weeks — that's all. What do you say?

Madeleine seems better tonight. We thank you for that. She's very sick, mind you, but never complains. There's pain, during the nights, and sometimes that's hard, even with the laudanum so if there was anything you could do. I hope this don't sound selfish but she's nearly all I got now and it would be very hard on me — if she — if she was to—

      GABRIEL cannot bring himself to say die.

                  ***

      Published by Coteau Books.

Of the Fields, Lately

David French

Ben Mercer comes home to Toronto in 1961 for his aunt's funeral, only to learn of his father's recent heart attack. His mother Mary and old family friend Wiff sustain the father, Jacob. Here Wiff talks to Mary about his dead wife Dot.

WIFF

I loved Dot, and don't you say I didn't. And she loved me, too. By Jesus, there was time I couldn't pass her chair without she'd reach out and touch me. And I was the same. I couldn't get close enough. I would've crawled down and lived inside her bowels. We was the perfect pair...

I never looked at another woman, including Marie, till Dot went t'rough the change of life. Wouldn't have a t'ing to do with me, after that. Too tired, she'd say. Always tired...

For crying out loud, Mary, I was on my way to the hospital, no odds what you believes. I wanted to say good-bye.
I just stopped off at the Oakwood for a minute. For a quick one, I told myself. I needed a good stiff drink right then, that's all there was to it. I'd been down to that hospital night after night for six weeks, watching her waste away to not'ing...hoping every day would be her last. I could hardly bear to look at her. One quick glass of Scotch. Should've only took two minutes, if that.

I had my first whiskey, and no sooner had I drunk it than somet'ing came back to me so clear. The first time Dot and me ever met. T'irty-five years ago. Me on my way down to the coal shed to unload the steamer, her on her way to the church to light the fire. How it all came back, suddenly, sitting at that table. That dark road, the stars still out, and me with my flashlight and lunchpail, no older than Ben. And who comes along the road towards me but Dot, the beam of her flashlight bouncing and swinging. I puts the light in her young face, and for a moment I don't recognize her, she's blossomed out that much in the time I was away in Boston...'Is that you, Dot Snow?' And she laughs. I'd forgot how gentle laughter could be. 'Is that you, Wiff Roach?' Well, duckie, I never made it to the coal shed that morning. No, by God, I never. And my father couldn't have dragged me, had he kicked me ass all the way with his biggest boots. I walked her up the road, instead, and we sat in her family pew till the sun come up. Two months later we was married. You remembers, Mary. You was the bridesmaid. (*slight pause*) So that's how come I never made it to the hospital yesterday. I had another whiskey to ease the pain I was feeling, and a t'ird because the second never helped...So if you wants to hurt me, Mary, you go right ahead, my dear, but you're too late...and not'ing you can ever say or do will make me feel any worse than knowing what Dot and me once had and what it come to in the end, without either one of us ever knowing why...and that's why I wants her buried in her wedding dress, if you must know, in spite of what she said at the last. What she wanted in those days past is just as real to me as what she wanted yesterday. Nor do it have the same sadness, Mary, not the same sadness at all...

***

Published by House of Anansi Press.

Acknowledgments to Drama Publishers

Playwrights Canada Press would like to thank the following publishers of Canadian drama for their kind permission to reprint monologues from their publications.

Coach House Press
760 Bathurst St.,
Toronto, ON
M5S 2R6
(416) 588-8999

Coteau Books
2206 Dewdney Ave., Suite 401,
Regina, SASK
S4R 1H3
(306) 777-0170

Fifth House Publishers
620 Duchess St.,
Saskatoon, SASK
S7K 0R1
(306) 242-4936

House of Anansi Press
1800 Steeles Ave., W.,
Concord, ON
L4K 2P3
(905) 660-0611

NeWest Press Publishers Ltd.,
10359-82 Ave., Suite 310,
Edmonton, AB
T6E 1Z9
(403) 432-9427

NuAge Editions
P.O. Box 8, Stn E,
Montréal, PQ
H2T 3A5
(514) 272-5226

Red Deer College Press
P.O. Box 5005, 56 Ave & 32 St.,
Red Deer, AB
T4N 5H5
(403) 342-3321

Scirocco Drama
P.O. Box 8, Stn E,
Montréal, PQ
H2T 3A5
(514) 272-5226

Talon Books Ltd.,
1019 East Cordova St., Suite 201
Vancouver, BC
V6A 1M8
(604) 253-5261

Index of Monologues

Index of Playwrights